Princeton Theological Monograph Series

Dikran Y. Hadidian

General Editor

38

HOW TO DO BIBLICAL THEOLOGY

17.00

How To Do Biblical Theology

PETER STUHLMACHER

PICKWICK PUBLICATIONS

An imprint of *Wipf and Stock Publishers*
199 West 8th Avenue • Eugene OR 97401

Pickwick Publications
A imprint of *Wipf and Stock Publishers*
199 West 8th Avenue, Suite 3
Eugene, Oregon 97401

How to do Biblical Theology
By Stuhlmacher, Peter

ISBN: 1-55635-026-0
Publication date 1/1/1995

Printed on Acid Free Paper in the United States of America

Library of Congress Cataloging-in-Publication Data

Stuhlmacher, Peter,
How to do Biblical Theology / Peter Stuhlmacher
p. cm. -- (Princeton theological monograph series ; 38)
Includes bibliographical references.)
ISBN 1-55635-026-0
1. Bible. N.T.--Theology 2. Bible. N.T. --Relation to the Old Testament. I. Title. II. Series.
BS2397.S874 1995
230--dc20

95-3730
CIP

To the Faculty of Theology
at the
University of Lund

Out of Gratitude for the Bestowal
of the
Doctor Honoris Causa

CONTENTS

PREFACE

In the fall of 1993 I was invited by Asbury Theological Seminary in Wilmore, Kentucky to deliver the Ryan Lectures, which were instituted by Rev. Dr. LOWELL RYAN and his late wife. The topic of these lectures was "How to do Biblical Theology." I spoke on this same subject at Yale Divinity School (New Haven, Connecticut) and then, in early 1994, before the Menighetsfaskultet in Oslo as well as at the School of Mission and Theology in Stavanger. DIKRAN Y. HADIDIAN of Pickwick Publications in Allison Park, Pennsylvania is to be thanked for agreeing to publish the English version of my lectures. The German version is to be published by Neukirchener Verlag, Neukirchen-Vluyn. I would like to dedicate both publications to the theological faculty in Lund (Sweden) as a sign of my sincere thanks for their bestowing upon me the honorary degree of Doctor of Theology on May 27, 1992.

Being involved with the task of Biblical Theology is a fascinating thing, but it is also not devoid of controversy. The longer I work in this area, the more it amazes and worries me that both the world of biblical scholarship and the Church no longer only accept with gratitude the biblical Word of God, but also continually rebel against its claims and authority. Since the primary duty of Biblical Theology is (in my opinion) to discover and develop the original historical meaning and the theological claims of the biblical texts, three secondary duties must be added. When interpreting the texts, she must attempt to follow a hermeneutic "which is characterized by an accepting acknowledgement, by historical self-identification, and by an acquisition of the reality" which the tradition reveals.[1] Second, she must always defend the text entrusted to her when it is obscured through historical or dogmatic misunderstanding. Finally, she should not be afraid to make use of theological criticism wherever it has been forgotten that the Protestant Churches—which are presently suffering through a severe identity crisis—only retain their right to exist over against the Catholic Churches as long as they earnestly seek to be and to remain *creatura verbi*.

I emphasize this because JÜRGEN ROLOFF in his review of the first volume of my "Biblische Theologie des Neuen Testaments" (in *ThLZ* 119, 1994, 241-245) has taken me to task for utilizing "historical hypotheses which are often daring and for the most part (at least anywhere else but in Tübingen) incapable of creating a consensus," in order to "prove the reliability of facts, the unbroken continuity of developments, and the unquestioned stability of traditions." His criticism ends with the question of whether "the unity of the New Testament is only to be had at the price of an apologetic which smooths over all historical tensions and perplexities?" (ibid. 245) I would, in all brevity, reply to this by making the three points.

1. ROLOFF's critique reflects a vexing problem which troubles especially German New Testament scholarship. With a few laudable exceptions, it has, since World War II, increasingly concentrated upon problems of interpretation relating to Systematic Theology, thus becoming ever more removed from solid philological and historical work. Because of this development, it is today very difficult to again attain a high level of competence in philological and historical matters as well. In light of this situation, it is a good thing when at least a few exegetes from the fields of Old and New Testament Studies (in Tübingen and in other places) again attempt to take up the historical duties of Biblical interpretation, without forgetting their obligation to provide a theological interpretation of the Holy Scriptures. To approach this in any other way would mean, as ROLOFF also points out, handing biblical exegesis over

to a historical positivism, fully untheological in nature, or to currents within so-called "postmodern" hermeneutics, for which even the mere assumption of an original historical meaning of texts has become meaningless.

2. The publication of the results of the Jesus Seminar, directed by ROBERT W. FUNK and JOHN DOMINIC CROSSAN, with the title *The Five Gospels—The Search for the Authentic Words of Jesus*. New Translation and Commentary by ROBERT W. FUNK, ROY W. HOOVER, and the JESUS SEMINAR, Macmillan Publishing Company, New York, 1993, documents how a group of exegetes from the U.S.A. have now gone to the other extreme. They celebrate the secularization of biblical exegesis as liberation, and using an objectifying historical method long outmoded, they investigate the four canonical Gospels and the so-called Gospel of Thomas with the goal of showing what Jesus really said and proving to what great degree his words and his whole work were altered and misrepresented after Easter. This undertaking represents a retrogression in hermeneutical reflection back to a point before the school of RUDOLF BULTMANN, and is a classic illustration of critical exegesis which, having liberated itself from all supposed ecclesiastical and theological constraints, succumbs to its own prejudices and false judgments. Instead of abandoning the biblical texts to this type of interpretation, thus contributing to the antagonism between a secular historical critical biblical interpretation and one which feels responsible to the Church and in which a critically differentiating exegesis of the Bible is completely dispensed with, Biblical Theology must insist that the biblical traditions be treated in a manner more suited to the texts, and also show that the picture which she sketches of, for example, the work of Jesus, is historically more illuminating and more meaningful for Christianity than is the artificial construction of the Jesus Seminar. When she functions in this way, then Biblical Theology does not practice the harmonizing apologetics as ROLOFF suspects, but protects the biblical tradition

from modern misunderstanding which disguises itself in historical critical dress.

3. As far as the unity of the New Testament is concerned, I have already emphasized in my article "Die Mitte der Schrift-biblisch-theologisch betrachtet"[2] (and in various places in the first volume of my Biblical Theology!) that which will become fully clear at the end of the second volume of my Theology: The unity of the New Testament, which cannot be separated from the Old, lies in God's gospel of Jesus Christ. From the very day that it was first proclaimed and taught it has produced controversy, not just among believers and unbelievers, but among Paul, Peter and James (cf. Gal 2:14; James 2:14-26) as well. If the unity of the New Testament and the Holy Scriptures lies fundamentally in the (always controversial) gospel, then the impression of apology which smooths over all rough spots can only arise when one does not make a historically exact inquiry into the origin and continuity of the New Testament proclamation of Christ. But if one asks oneself how it is possible that, despite the undeniable differences in the witnesses, the gospel came to be so clearly formulated and handed down, first in Jerusalem, but soon also in Damascus, Antioch and Rome, then, above all, in the school of Paul, and finally in the Johannine circle, that the ancient Church could venture to bring the various biblical voices together into one canon of scriptures and a "rule of faith," (*regula fidei*) then the view of the different New Testament formulations of tradition which I have proposed are much more plausible than ROLOFF cares to believe.

The points of contention which ROLOFF has touched upon could only be finally settled when a small group got together and again attempted to consider what historical scholarship actually can and cannot do within a biblical context, how the New Testament concept of tradition is structured, and what it means to speak with Paul of the "truth of the gospel" (Gal 2:14). A symposium dealing with such issues would most certainly be difficult, but would be just as certainly a beneficial and thus worthwhile exercise!

GERLINDE EISENKOLB and HANNASTETTLER read the manuscripts and compiled the bibliographic references. JONATHAN M. WHITLOCK translated the lectures into English, and SCOTT HAFEMANN contributed a manuscript, in which he traces the development of my attempts to understand the biblical expression "righteousness of God" and my involvement in Biblical Theology as a whole. I owe them all my deepest thanks for their efforts and cooperation.

Tübingen, Germany
September, 1994

Peter Stuhlmacher

1. H. Gese, "Hermeneutische Grundsätze der Exegese biblischer Texte," in his *Alttestamentliche Studien,* 1991, pp. 249-265 (cit. 265).

2. In *Wissenschaft und Kirche*, FS for E. Lohse, (eds.) K. ALAND and S. MEURER, 1989, pp. 29-56.

THE "RIGHTEOUSNESS OF GOD"

An Introduction to the Theological and Historical Foundation of Peter Stuhlmacher's Biblical Theology of the New Testament[1]

Scott Hafemann
Gordon-Conwell Theological Seminary

Dr. Peter Stuhlmacher has been Professor of New Testament at the University of Tübingen for over 20 years. During this time, his scholarship has not only been vast, but encyclopedic in its theological and exegetical scope. His study ranges from the letters of Paul to the life of Jesus, from a critique of historical criticism to his own proposal for a hermeneutic adequate to deal with the New Testament, from the meaning of a given verse to the structure of biblical theology viewed in its totality. A prolific writer, his current works in English translation include *Historical Criticism and Theological Interpretation of Scripture* (1977); *Paul: Rabbi and Apostle* (with Pinchas Lapide, 1984); *Reconciliation, Law and Righteousness: Essays in Biblical Theology* (1986); *The Gospel and the Gospels* (1991), which he edited; *Jesus of Nazareth, Christ of Faith* (1994); and most recently, *Paul's Letter to the Romans, A Commentary* (1994). Finally, Prof. Stuhlmacher's ongoing development of a biblical theology of the New Testament has culminated in the first of a two volume study entitled, *Biblische Theologie des Neuen Testaments, Band 1: Grundlegung: Von Jesus zu Paulus* (1992).

The following essays outline the basic principles which undergird Stuhlmacher's approach to formulating a biblical theology of the New Testament and thus offer the

English reader an introduction to the overall framework of his thought. Rather than tracing the arguments presented in the following essays themselves, the purpose of this introduction is to provide the reader with the theological and historical foundation upon which Stuhlmacher's biblical theology of the New Testament has been built. In doing so, it endeavors to help the reader evaluate the wider context within which the following essays find their home, in order that one might understand and pass judgment on them more adequately. For throughout Stuhlmacher's study and teaching, there has been one recurring theme which ties his biblical-theological work together and gives it coherence, namely, the righteousness of the one God who created the world and chose Israel to be his people (Exod 20:1-6; Deut 6:4-5; Hos 11:8-9; Isa 7:9; 43:1-7; 52:13-52:12; Jer 31:31-34; Ps 139:117; etc.), which has now been revealed through the Gospel of justification by faith (Rom1:16f.) as this was made possible by the life and death of Christ (Mark 10:45; 14:22, 24; Rom 3:21-31; 4:25; 2 Cor 5:21; John 11:25-26; 1 John 2:1-2; 4:9-10, etc.). As the fourth essay in this volume makes clear, for Stuhlmacher the center of the canon is found in the witness to this fundamental truth.

Indeed, the pivotal role that the righteousness of God plays in providing the impetus and framework for Stuhlmacher's exegetical and theological labors is clear from the very beginning of his scholarly career. In the preface to the published version of his 1962 Tübingen dissertation, Stuhlmacher acknowledged that his study of the "righteousness" terminology in Paul was not to be undertaken for its own sake, but was "merely a first step on the way to a new understanding of the Pauline theology of justification."[2] Moreover, he also recognized that in order to carry out this new interpretation it would be necessary

> to work out entirely new categories which still
> allow the dogmatic legitimacy of the traditional
> distinction between imputed and effective
> justification to be maintained,
> but nevertheless express justification

> in terms of the free and comprehensive act of creation which Paul sees it to be.[3]

It is the working out of these new categories, together with their implications for the relationship between the imputed and effective righteousness of God in the theology of the New Testament, which, more than anything else, have provided the framework for the last 30 years of Prof. Stuhlmacher's interpretive work.

The Righteousness of God in Paul's Thought as the Theological Foundation for Stuhlmacher's Biblical Theology of the New Testament

The foundation for this new understanding of the righteousness of God was laid in the 1966 revised form of Stuhlmacher's dissertation, *Gerechtigkeit Gottes bei Paulus* (The Righteousness of God in Paul's Thought). This study took its bearings from the essay of the same name by his Doktorvater, Ernst Käsemann, and from the recently published thesis of Chr. Müller, *Gottes Gerechtigkeit und Gottes Volk. Eine Untersuchung zu Röm 9-11* (God's Righteousness and God's People, An investigation of Rom 9-11), since Stuhlmacher saw these works as opening the way in the modern discussion for rethinking the righteousness of God in Paul's thought (p. 69).[4] First, it was significant that independent of his own work and in agreement with Stuhlmacher's thesis, Müller had argued that Romans 9-11 "was based upon an eschatological creation-tradition which was forensically conceived and that this creation-tradition constituted the essential nature of the Pauline doctrine of justification" (p. 69). It was this realization that allowed Romans to be understood as a unity, without having to relegate chapters 9-11 to a parenthetical excursus, a perspective which Stuhlmacher has now carried through in detail in his recent commentary on Romans. Moreover, Müller argued, as Stuhlmacher's own study developed in great detail, that Paul's understanding of the righteousness of God was "dependent upon the Old Testament concept of the cosmic lawsuit, which was then further extended in apocalyptic literature" (p. 69). Moreover, of these two traditions, Stuhlmacher argued, based on the fact that the righteousness-terminology occurs in the OT only in Deut 33:21 (cf. pp. 73, 109), that it was the apocalyptic writings which ought to receive our "special attention" (pp. 73, 109). Hence, the righteousness of God in Paul's thought is to be understood as the " 'eschatological realization of the justice of God toward the world' " (p. 69, quoting Müller). In fundamental agreement with this conclusion, Stuhlmacher's question became whether Müller had established clearly enough the antithetical contrast between the "wrath of God" and the "righteousness of God" in the sense portrayed in Rom 1:17f, so that the justice of God could be understood primarily, if not exclusively, as a redeeming act of liberation (p. 69). Stuhlmacher's comments on Paul's calling in his third essay in this volume draw out the implications of this understanding for Paul's own experience of justification.

Second, although Stuhlmacher himself would later come to modify his views in this regard (see p. xxviiif.), it was his initial conviction concerning the antithetical relationship between the righteousness of God and the wrath of God which also led him to argue that although Käsemann's view pointed the way forward, it too had to be supplemented and revised. Nevertheless, Stuhlmacher's own study substantiated Käsemann's assertion that the righteousness of God "is an independent technical term with its own history of tradition within Judaism, which begins with Deut 33:21 and then once again appears in the Qumran texts (cf. pp. 102-184). Hence, methodologically, the meaning of the phrase δικαιοσύνη θεοῦ (= "righteousness of God") is no longer to be determined on the basis of the general (Greek) concept of δικαιοσύνη (= "righteousness")" (p. 69; cf. p. 73). Indeed, as Stuhlmacher's survey of the history of the interpretation of δικαιοσύνη in Paul made clear, "Up until now Greek judicial categories have always led . . . to an ambiguity concerning the concept which does not appear to be of significance in the texts themselves" (p. 73). In contrast, Stuhlmacher's own work was intended to demonstrate that "only the Old Testament and Jewish judicial categories appear to be appropriate to the concept δικαιοσύνη θεοῦ and its interpretation"(p.73).[5] The priority here given to the biblical and Jewish post-biblical tradition as the key to understanding Paul's concept of the righteousness of God thus established one of the central methodological principles for Stuhlmacher's biblical theology of the New Testament as a whole. Third, Stuhlmacher followed Käsemann's postulate that the "righteousness of God" was for Paul a "concept which encompassed both power and gift" and that, in contrast to the pre-Pauline tradition which he inherited and reinterpreted, it no longer referred merely to God's faithfulness to his covenant, but included " 'the divine faithfulness in regard to God's relationship . . . toward the entire creation' " (p. 70, quoting in the latter reference, Käsemann, pp. 374f.). Moreover, Käsemann's emphasis on the fact that God's faithfulness to his creation compelled his addressees into its service, so that Paul can speak of a "bondage to righteousness"in Rom 6:1ff., Rom 12-14, and 2 Cor 3:9, etc., certainly pointed one in the right direction (p. 70).

Finally, Stuhlmacher's own work, both in his dissertation and throughout the next 30 years, would serve to strengthen the conviction also held by Käsemann that the righteousness of God is the central theme of the entire preaching and theology of Paul (p. 70). This too becomes a central pillar in his biblical theology of the NT as testified to in the present work.

But if these perspectives were true, then Stuhlmacher observed that the link in Paul's thought between the Spirit as the power and presence of God and the righteousness of God must be given greater prominence than Käsemann had done (p. 70). For in the final analysis, Käsemann himself did not break clean from the common attempt to interpret the righteousness of God against the backdrop of the Greek tradition of justice, in which the righteousness of God referred not only to God's salvific work, but also to "a punishing activity on behalf of God" (p. 70). As with Müller, the question here too thus became whether the wrath and judgment of God are also expressions of God's righteousness. But if not, how then can the twin themes of God's righteousness as the right of God which establishes itself in the world and as the demonstration of the creator who considers not only his own right, but also in a more profound way the salvation of those who belong to him, be brought together into a unity?

The search for an answer to these two fundamental questions became the burden of Stuhlmacher's dissertation, in which he argued that throughout Paul's letters, "when he spoke of the δικαιοσύνη θεοῦ (= the "righteousness of God") Paul took over an apocalyptic technical term which he could then elevate to the central concept of his theology, since it reflected an eschatology which, like his own, was still characterized by an apocalyptic perspective and as such was part of a world view which also corresponded to this same apocalyptic framework" (p. 71). The key to Paul's thinking, therefore, was the realization that it was this apocalyptic tradition which most directly provided both the thoroughgoing eschatological world view and conceptual framework for Paul's understanding of the righteousness of God (cf. 56f., 60, 72f.). For in the literature of apocalyptic Judaism, including the Qumran writings, not only was the righteousness of God a technical term, but its reference was clearly to "God's own conduct, God's justice, whereby God's creative activity, his faithfulness to the covenant and his forgiving mercy are to be conceptualized together with his demand for obedience" (p. 175). Furthermore, "in apocalyptic thought one must also speak ontologically of a correspondence between the power of the word and the power of creation and thus understand the righteousness of God as the power of the creative word of God..."(p.175).

At this point, Stuhlmacher's indebtedness to Käsemann's emphasis on the central role which apocalyptic thinking plays in NT theology is apparent, an indebtedness that paved the way for the messianic perspective of Stuhlmacher's later biblical theology as outlined in these essays (see especially chapters two and four). For in his later studies Stuhlmacher would revise his earlier attempt to make a clean break between the Old Testament and early Jewish apocalyptic literature, since he came to see it as introducing a distinction where none exists.[6] This emphasis on the theological continuity between the Old Testament, the so-called intertestamental literature of postbiblical Judaism, and the New Testament now finds expression in his corresponding stress on the openness and unity of the *canonical* process stretching from the OT to the NT, a point which is fundamental to his understanding of the relationship between the Testaments (see chapters one and five below). Moreover, in response to subsequent criticism concerning the one-sidedness of his early formulations, Stuhlmacher also came to see that it was not possible to maintain a stark alternative between the righteousness of God as God's own "justice" or "right"*(Recht)* and as the righteousness granted to his people (see p. xxix). However, Stuhlmacher has remained unconvinced of the equally one-sidedness of his critics who argue "that God's righteousness in Paul's thought has above all the meaning of the righteousness of faith and see in this the specific contribution of the Pauline conception of righteousness over against the pre-Pauline tradition."[7] In his view, this interpretation is supported neither by the Old Testament and Jewish tradition, nor by the history of tradition from Jesus to Paul, but derives rather from the Lutheran "stamp" *(Prägung)* of his critics.[8] In his recent Romans commentary, Stuhlmacher has thus once again affirmed that in the OT, as in the Jewish literature and Qumran texts which are based upon it, that ". . . God's righteousness thus means the activity of God through which he creates well-being and salvation in history (specifically that of Israel), in creation, and in the situation of the earthly or eschatological judgment."[9]

This comprehensive definition of the righteousness of God both in the OT and in Paul, together with his stress on the unity of the pre-Pauline and Pauline traditions concerning the righteousness of God, provide two more of the basic pillars of Stuhlmacher's biblical theology of the NT. Taken together they support his conviction that there is a theological center and unity to the NT canon which is focused around the messianic identity and work of Christ (see chapters one and four). For armed with this same perspective from apocalyptic literature, Stuhlmacher had already argued in his dissertation that the righteousness of God in Paul's thought could be understood in a unified sense once it was realized that for Paul the new age of the righteousness of God had already broken in proleptically with Christ. Rather than referring merely, or even primarily, to the result of a forensic transaction in *heaven* which transcends time (as in Luther's definition of the righteousness of God as the "righteousness, which is valid before God"), Paul could speak of the reality of the righteousness of God *in the lives of God's people* precisely because God's power to save and vindicate, in accordance with his faithfulness to his covenant, was already being poured out in the*world* through Christ. In 2 Cor 5:21, rather than being a reference to the gift of God, the righteousness of God can thus even refer to "a state of being determined by a power, here designated with the name of the power which determines it, namely, the δικαιοσύνη θεοῦ (= the "righteousness of God")" (p. 75; cf. p. 77).

The point of Rom 1:17, therefore, is that "God's manifestation of his justice, which creates anew, has broken into the old world and has begun its triumphal procession" (p. 84). In Rom 3:4f. "δικαιοσύνη θεοῦ (= "the righteousness of God") stands in parallel to πίστις θεοῦ (= "faithfulness of God") and ἀλήθεια θεοῦ (= "truth of God") and means God's own trustworthy adherence to his (covenantal) justice as confirmed in his lawsuit" (p. 86). In the same way, in Rom 3:21-26 the righteousness of God is again the salvific "creative power of God," this time clearly seen in the eschatological "inauguration of God's new world in the saving sacrifice of Christ" as that which makes possible "the covenant faithfulness of God which brings about forgiveness" (pp. 87-89; see chapter two below for Stuhlmacher's corresponding understanding of the passion of Christ as foundational to his biblical theology). But as Rom 3:26 makes clear, "if . . . Paul no longer merely aligns God and the covenant to one another, but also God and the world, then δικαιοσύνη θεοῦ (= the "righteousness of God") can no longer mean for him simply faithfulness to his covenant, as in v. 25, but must refer to the faithfulness of the creator to his creation, which, duly noted, takes place as an event of justice!" (p. 90). Hence, "throughout the entire paragraph of Rom 3:21-26 δικαιοσύνη θεοῦ (= the "righteousness of God") . . . again designates simply God's own salvific justice, God's *worldwide* faithfulness as creator"(p.91, emphasis mine). Likewise, in Rom 10:3, "in accordance with the verb ἀγνοέω (= "to be ignorant"), δικαιοσύνη θεοῦ (= the "righteousness of God") must refer to the power of God which is active as the eschatological and authoritative might of the creator which directs history and its destiny, i.e. to God's own conduct. Only with this interpretation does the phrase (= οὐχ ὑπετάγησαν "they did not submit") take on a precise meaning. For this verb means to submit under the divine and authoritative will and power . . . this will and power is designated with the phrase δικαιοσύνη θεοῦ (= the "righteousness of God") (p. 93).

For Stuhlmacher, therefore, the righteousness of God in Paul's thought (and later argued to be the case in the NT as a whole!) is first and foremost the power of God which brings one into the new world of the kingdom of God, which, in turn, is made possible by the "forensic situation" brought about by the cross of Christ and realized in the world through participation in the body of Christ (p. 76). As a result, Stuhlmacher could begin to solve the tension between the theological categories of imputed and effective righteousness by emphasizing that "the ontological bridge which makes the Pauline statements possible is the concept of the πνεῦμα (= Spirit)" (p. 76). Hence, contra the view of A. Schweitzer and those who follow him even today,[10] rather than being in conflict or distinct from one another, for Paul mystic union with Christ and justification are bound together into one conceptual unity (p. 75 n.3).

What then is justification? Once again it is not primarily a forensic act in heaven which transcends time. Instead, it is the eschatological saving act of God on behalf of his people and by his power in which they are freed from the power of sin and incorporated by means of the Spirit into the body of Christ (cf. pp. 75f., 99). As a result, the one who believes is forgiven in the present and is already a part of Christ's body. At the same time, the believer also looks forward to the future judgment as one who has been empowered and enabled to stand in it by the power of Christ's resurrection and by virtue of being "in Christ." This is the point of Phil 3:9, where, "using the language of justification, Paul describes the change from a Jewish to a Christian self-understanding and the incorporation into the body of Christ which takes place in baptism"(p. 99). For this reason, justification and the pouring out of the Spirit in one's life are "simply parallel designations for one and the same state of affairs" (p.100). Fifteen years later Stuhlmacher would put it this way in his essay, "Die Gerechtigkeitsanschauung des Apostels Paulus": "In Paul's thought 'justification' therefore designates both the participation in God's grace already obtained in faith as well as the acquittal before God in the final judgment," which Paul described as a "new life" received at baptism, maintained in one's "service to righteousness"(Rom 6:18), and completed with one's participation in the resurrected glory of Christ (Phil 3:20f.).[11] Stuhlmacher consequently concludes that "if one takes Paul at his word, then the justification of which he speaks is a process of becoming new which spans the earthly life of every believer, a pathway from obtaining faith to the consummation of faith."[12] It is this realization that the righteousness of God is both an eschatological and ontological reality, and that it is this reality which determines the character of God's people, that overcomes the tension between the classical distinction between imputed and effective righteousness. And again, that which spans this tension is the work and reality of the Spirit as the power of God in the lives of believers. This is the point implied in Phil 3:9, where we now encounter the expression δικαιοσύνη ἐκ θεοῦ (="righteousness *from* God"). In Stuhlmacher's view, in this text

> Paul designates judicial acceptance before God in the judgment and the reality of a new creaturely position with ἡ ἐκ θεοῦ δικαιοσύνη (= "the righteousness from God"), as a result of taking up an expression from Isa 54:17. That this righteousness concerns not only a forensic acceptance in the final judgment, but a new position in God's world, is signaled by the concept of the Spirit which stands in the background of the verse. For it is the Spirit which in reality bestows on one participation in the being of Christ. This bestowing of the Spirit and the declaration that one is righteous are one and the same occurrence, namely, the invasion of God's power as creator (= δικαιοσύνη θεοῦ [= the "righteousness of God"]). Hence, . . . according to Phil 3:9, judicial and mystical doctrines of redemption cannot be separated. God's faithfulness as creator is a salvific δικαιοσύνη (= "righteousness"), its individuation is the δικαιοσύνη ἐκ θεοῦ (="righteousness from God"). This is why, in Paul's thought, the gift of divine righteousness is only indicated terminologically in those places where soteriology comes into view, that is, only in relationship to the question of justification (pp. 100f.).

This unified understanding of the righteousness of God in Paul, which is seen to be the "governing motif for Pauline eschatology, for his Christology, his understanding of the Church, and naturally for his doctrine of justification" (p. 203), is the *theological* foundation upon which Stuhlmacher's biblical theology of the New Testament as a whole is built.

*The Righteousness of God in the Life and Teaching of Jesus as the **Historical** Foundation for a Biblical Theology of the New Testament*

From this point on, Stuhlmacher's work, culminating in his biblical theology, can be seen as a continuing refinement and development of his understanding of the meaning and centrality of the righteousness of God not only in Paul's thought, but in the theology of the rest of the New Testament as well, consistently interpreted against the backdrop of the Old Testament and postbiblical Judaism. Essential to this development is his subsequent work on the history of the biblical traditions concerning righteousness and its related themes in regard to the historical Jesus as reflected in the Synoptic Gospels. For chapter two below makes clear that in Stuhlmacher's view a biblical theology of the New Testament can only be adequately formulated when the current scholarly skepticism concerning the fundamental trustworthiness of the Synoptic tradition is overcome and the attempt to reconstruct an "historical Jesus" behind the gospels is abandoned. In his dissertation, Stuhlmacher had argued that Paul, "influenced by the early Christian doctrine of justification, had elevated 'God's righteousness' to the central concept of his theology as a result of having *independently* reached back to the conception of justification found in late apocalyptic Judaism and in continuity with apocalyptic thought" (p. 187, emphasis mine). But later he came to see that *historically* there was an unbroken line of tradition stretching from the OT to Jesus, and from Jesus, through the early church, to Paul.[13] As the following essays in this volume illustrate so well, it is this conviction concerning the unity of the early Christian tradition that provides the framework for developing a biblical theology of the *entire* New Testament.

At the heart of this new picture of the unity of the early Christian tradition, beginning with Jesus himself, was Stuhlmacher's reexamination of Jesus' messianic self-understanding as the Son of Man as this crystallized in Mark 10:45, which he convincingly argued on historical grounds was authentic.[14] Hence, as the Son of Man from Dan 7:13ff. (cf. 1 Enoch 45-62 and 4 Ezra 13), Jesus knew himself to be the one sent as the judge of the world to establish the rule of God's kingdom. Stuhlmacher thus came to posit that "for Jesus, who followed the call to repentance of John the Baptist, 'holiness and righteousness before God' (Luke 1:74f.), and the worldwide order of the righteousness of God, which will be brought about by the Son of Man-Messiah in the final judgment, were inescapable themes" (emphasis mine).[15] Indeed, "it was impossible for any Jew of the New Testament period to conceive of the rule of God without thinking of God's righteousness which characterizes this rule.[16]

As a result, "Jesus took his stand concerning these themes and *with his entire way of life paved the way for a new understanding of God's righteousness and of righteousness before God.*"[17] As chapter two below therefore emphasizes, the biblical theology of the early church and of Paul finds its roots in the fact that Jesus saw in his own work the breaking in of the kingdom of God (Luke 11:20; 6:20; 17:20f., etc.). Yet as Mark 10:45 makes clear, once it is read against the backdrop of Isa 43:3f. and 53:10-12, the shocking thing about Jesus in his role as the messianic Son of Man is that he does not deny the judgment of God which accompanies the coming of God's kingdom and its righteousness, but willingly takes it upon himself, rather than bestowing it on those who deserve it.[18] Jesus' call of the disciples, his messianic work in fulfillment of Isa 61:1f, and his table fellowship with tax collectors and sinners consequently not only extended the kingdom of God to unexpected recipients, but also demonstrated that those whom God "justifies" (see Luke 18:13), he also "enables . . . as the gracious judge to a new right of existence by means of forgiveness."[19] In Luke 18:13 "Jesus formulates . . . in narrative form the principle of the justification of sinners . . . God's righteousness is for Jesus more than merely a judicial activity which determines reward and punishment; by means of the forgiveness of sins the righteous God enables the repentant person to a new life."[20]

Viewed from this perspective, the righteousness of God made possible by the representative and atoning death of Christ, which brings new life and enables a new way of life, carries with it a necessary call to obey the will of God. Rather than preaching a "cheap grace," the righteousness of God brought, preached, and exemplified by Jesus leads to the conclusion that in Jesus' teaching and messianic work, "those who will one day stand before the judge of the world will receive salvation on the basis of whether or not they have genuinely accepted their fellow men and women in their suffering and need."[21] Thus, here too the tension between imputed and effective righteousness is bridged, once the concept of the righteousness of God is seen to encompass not only forgiveness, but the power for a new life lived on behalf of others.

It was this inextricable link between justification and sanctification in the ministry, death, and resurrection of Jesus, based on the liberating power of God's work in and through his messianic life, which then became the basis of the Pauline gospel as well. According to Stuhlmacher, such a link can be seen in the tie between Rom l:l-5 and 1:17, in 1 Cor 1:30, and in the early Christian "atonement tradition" based on Jesus' own self-understanding now preserved in Rom 3:21-26 and 4:5.[22] In basic agreement with his dissertation, Stuhlmacher can thus continue to define the righteousness of God in Rom 1:17 as the "summarizing concept (*Inbegriff*) of the salvific work of God in Christ which, within the horizon of judgment, brings about new life for those who believe."[23] This Stuhlmacher finds confirmed throughout the other relevant Pauline passages, where, in a "synthetic" way that is typical of Old Testament terminology, Paul follows the early Christian practice of using the righteousness of God to refer both to God's own "judicial acts" as well as to the result of this activity.[24]

Unlike his dissertation, however, he now maintains

that the righteousness of God in Rom 3:5 also refers to God's own righteousness, "by virtue of which he pronounces a judgment of wrath on the unrighteousness of mankind."[25] By doing so, Stuhlmacher now associates God's wrath as well with the righteousness of God, whereas earlier he viewed the wrath of God and the righteousness of God to be in opposition to one another.[26] Indeed, in regard to Rom 3:5 Stuhlmacher can even speak of God's "righteousness as judge" *(Richtergerechtigkeit)*.[27] Here too, Stuhlmacher understands the historical basis for this view to be the cross itself, understood as a "punishing judgment" (*Strafgericht*) which derives from, though does not exhaust, God's righteousness.[28] Nevertheless, Rom 3:3f. indicates, as part of the same context, that "for the apostle the expression 'God's righteousness' retained the nuance of a positive quality, even within the horizon of judgment," since in the Old Testament the righteousness of God in juridical contexts refers directly to the vindication of the righteous, and only indirectly to the corresponding and implied judgment of the wicked.[29] Concerning this positive side, the righteousness of God in Rom 3:25-26 is that which works life for the lost, while in 3:21-22 it is "at the same time the righteousness of faith which makes itself accessible to sinners on the basis of this salvific work of God in Christ."[30] Thus, here too "justification" clearly carries the "dimension of new creation."[31] It is this "synthetic" understanding of the "righteousness of God" which continues to bridge the gap between the traditional conception of God's righteousness as either imputed or effective. Both are present, and it is merely a matter of determining from context to context where the accent lies.[32] Hence, in a critique of his earlier work, Stuhlmacher pointed to the fact that in it he had "handled . . . the concept of God's righteousness too rigidly as a fixed *terminus technicus* which always has only the meaning of God's own justice."[33] For in reality, as summarized recently in Stuhlmacher's Romans commentary,

> The one expression, "the righteousness of God," was already understood in the Christian tradi-

> tion which existed before Paul to refer at the same time both to God's own salvific activity (Rom 3:25f.) and to its effect in the form of the righteousness which is allotted to those who, in faith, confess Christ (2 Cor 5:21) . . . In the Old Testament, in the early Jewish tradition, and in the New Testament, God's righteousness thus means the salvific activity of God the creator and judge, who creates for those concerned righteousness and well-being . . . But in Paul's gospel this righteousness of God is already being revealed before the beginning of the day of judgment and made possible for those who believe.[34]

It is this comprehensive view of the righteousness of God, based on the teaching of Jesus himself (!) and grounded in the traditions of the Old Testament and post-biblical Judaism, which thus becomes the foundation for constructing a biblical theology of the entire NT. Conversely, as the following essays make clear, the goal of such a biblical theology is to trace the tradition from Jesus to Paul, and from Jesus to the logos-tradition of the Johannine writings. We must await Stuhlmacher's second volume to see how the Johannine tradition as a whole and the rest of the NT will be incorporated into this framework.

Evaluating Stuhlmacher's Biblical Theology of the New Testament

In order to evaluate Stuhlmacher's following proposal concerning the formulation of a biblical theology of the New Testament, it becomes necessary to offer a few basic observations concerning the significance of Stuhlmacher's work on the righteousness of God within the context of the history of the interpretation of this theme.[35] For as Stuhlmacher's own method of working and hermeneutic make clear,[36] it is only in dialogue with the history of the interpretation of a text that the original intention of the biblical text and its implications come to light. Hence, when the theological and historical foundation of Stuhlmacher's biblical theology is examined in the light of his own analysis of the history of the interpretation of the righteousness of God in Paul as presented in his dissertation,[37] the following perspectives emerge.

First, Stuhlmacher's ongoing concern with the theme of "the righteousness of God" has been brought about by the historical and theological necessity of a re-evaluation of the theme itself the initial impetus and framework for Stuhlmacher's work was provided by the then recent works of Jeremias, Michel, Müller, and, above all, his own *Doktorvater* Ernst Käsemann (cf. pp. 66-70). But his own study of the history of its interpretation led to the serious recognition that "in the almost two thousand year long history of its interpretation . . . the phenomenon designated by Paul with the phrase δικαιοσύνη θεοῦ (= "righteousness of God"), and as a result the Pauline doctrine of justification as well, has only seldom been sharply recognized and precisely understood theologically" (p. 71). The reason for this lack of clarity was that the history of interpretation had failed to understand the righteousness of God in Paul's thought against its proper *religionsgeschichtliche* background and within the ancient worldview in which Paul himself lived and thought (p. 11; cf. pp. 71-73). In response, Stuhlmacher's own synthetic understanding of the righteousness of God seeks to bridge the gap between the understanding of God's righteousness as "imputed" and as "real" or "effective" by overcoming the past attempts to look for the center of Paul's thought either in a forensic view of the righteousness of God or in the concept of a mystical union "in Christ." The key to such a reconceptualization is to anchor Paul's thought in the worldview which he inherited from the OT and post-biblical Judaism on the one hand, and in the life and teachings of Jesus on the other. To do so paves the way for a biblical theology of the NT in which the central themes of the righteousness of God on behalf of his creation and of the justification of both Jews and Gentiles before God's judgment are brought together in harmony. Stuhlmacher can thus argue for a center in the

NT canon where most see only a diversity of (even contradictory!) emphases. Regardless of how one evaluates his interpretation of the meaning of the righteousness of God itself, therefore, Stuhlmacher's insistence on Jesus, Judaism, and the OT as the interpretive "religionsgeschichtliche" keys to the theology of the NT is a crucial step forward.

Second, Stuhlmacher's dissertation study of the uncertainty and misunderstandings surrounding the meaning of the righteousness of God in the history of scholarship eventually led to his own advocacy of a "hermeneutic of 'sympathetic understanding' (*Einverständnis*)" for approaching biblical texts.[38] Such an approach seeks first and foremost to read the Scriptures within the historical and theological context in which they were written, with empathy, before submitting them to an external criticism concerning their content (*Sachkritik*). Only in this way can a genuine biblical theology be produced. Here too, Stuhlmacher's caution that all study of the Scriptures must begin with the attempt to understand them on their own terms is to be heeded. For Stuhlmacher's historical survey illustrated how quickly the Church lost the ability to understand Paul because of her acceptance of a non-Pauline eschatology on the one hand, and because of her loss of a Pauline ontology on the other. Instead of Paul's eschatological conviction concerning the present overlapping of the ages, with its corresponding tension between the present and the future, the Apostolic Fathers and the history of tradition which they founded held only to a more or less prolonged expectation for the future (p. 12). As a result, that aspect of Paul's thought which focused on the nature of one's works before the future judgment of God came to dominate the theology of the Fathers, so that the present experience of the righteousness of God as understood by Paul was lost. And in place of Paul's pessimistic anthropology, an optimism concerning mankind's ability to prepare for this judgment emerged under the growing influence of Hellenistic thought (p. 12). It was this non-Pauline ontology and eschatology which kept the Church from adequately understanding Paul until the Reformation (p.14 n.1). Only then was Paul's eschatology and ontology brought back together in such a way that a renewed understanding of Paul's doctrine of justification could be gained.[39] In the same way, modern historical-criticism, with its doctrinaire anti-supernaturalism and sense of cultural and philosophical superiority, also runs the risk of blinding us to the biblical texts today.

Third, Stuhlmacher's commitment to constructing a biblical theology of the New Testament can also be seen to be rooted in his early work concerning the righteousness of God. Already in his dissertation, Stuhlmacher saw that by the time of F. Chr. Baur the resurgence of Greek legal categories within the exegetical tradition (cf. e.g. the work of Bengel and J. J. Wettstein), the dominance of rationalism as a worldview, and the control of orthodoxy had made it all but impossible to find one's way back to Luther not to mention to Paul himself (cf. pp. 27-29). Once again, the root cause of this inability was simple: the history of interpretation still lacked the proper OT and Jewish "history of religions" backdrop for understanding Paul (cf. p. 37). Today, such an analysis seems obvious. Indeed, apart from a few remaining pockets of the old Bultmannian perspective, NT scholarship over the last twenty years has become pervasively convinced that the Old Testament scriptures and post-biblical Judaism are in fact the essential background for understanding the New Testament.[40] But already as a doctoral student in the early 1960s Stuhlmacher was convinced that the breakthrough to a new understanding of the righteousness of God "succeeds only where God's righteousness is seen in the context of Pauline eschatology and, at the same time, is investigated in accordance with the (proper) history of religion roots of the concept, whereby the dominance of the Greek judicial way of thinking can now finally be broken" (pp. 37f.). As a further extension of this principle, Stuhlmacher's program of developing a biblical theology of the New Testament seeks to free the text to speak once again in and from its own appropriate historical, theological, and eschatological context.

Finally, Stuhlmacher's subsequent conviction concerning the possibility of uncovering a unifying center of the New Testament, as well as his delineation of it, are a working out of his rejection of contemporary attempts to develop a theology exclusively either from "below," or from "above." Already in his dissertation, Stuhlmacher rejected Bultmann's attempt to make anthropology the sole subject of theology. Bultmann's corresponding program of demythologizing the future aspects of Paul's apocalyptic eschatology for the sake of the present had forced him to offer "in principle only the unsatisfying traditional dichotomy of the concept (of righteousness) into two distinct meanings," with the righteousness of God equated primarily with the present gift of God's "declaration of acquittal" (pp. 55f.). Here too the lack of an understanding of Paul's eschatological framework led to a truncated view of Paul's thought. The inadequacy of Bultmann's position was then confirmed by his inability to incorporate Paul's statements concerning the final judgment according to one's works, which Christians must also endure, into his purely forensic theological scheme (cf.1 Cor1:8; 2:12-15; 4:4f; 2 Cor 5: 10; 1 Thess 3:13; 5:23). Because Bultmann fails to bring together the doctrines of creation and justification, all he can do with such statements is to view them as a "Jewish remnant" left over in Paul's thinking and push them aside (p. 57).

On the other hand, the following essays make clear that Stuhlmacher is indebted to Karl Barth for his theological starting point. Yet as a doctoral student he had already voiced reservations concerning Barth's attempts to come to grips with the righteousness of God in Paul's thought solely from the perspective of theology proper. In view of the apocalyptic character of his own time, Barth's concern became the "*self* justification of God" as that which includes the justification of the creature, since God is the creator (p. 57, emphasis mine). Barth could thus declare that "God's righteousness means the right (*Recht*) of God as observed by God in Christ."[41] As a result, he interpreted the righteousness of God in Rom 10:3 to be 'the freedom of God to establish himself as the norm, i.e. his freedom to be the one who calls in and of himself, upon whom everything depends.' "[42] But Stuhlmacher argued that not only did such a definition derive from an abstract speculation concerning God, rather than from an exegesis of Paul, it also demonstrated that "Barth . . ., despite his protest against the use of Aristotelian categories in the interpretation of righteousness, could not free himself entirely from Greek legal categories of thought" (p. 58). Moreover, the way in which Barth moved directly from a theological view of justification to one's political responsibility "presupposes a present validity of God's righteousness in a way that, within the framework of Pauline eschatology, is precisely not yet the case. For Paul, God is still in the process of procuring the validity of his righteousness in the struggle against the powers of the old age . . . The sacrifice of Christ in Rom 3:24f., offered by God himself, is also not yet—as Barth would very much like it to be—God's invasion of power plain and simple, but merely the inauguration of the eschatological manifestation of God's justice!" (p. 58, emphasis mine). Like Bultmann, Barth too thus had an over-realized eschatology, though in the opposite direction.

In contrast, Stuhlmacher's biblical theology of the New Testament is rightly characterized by the recognition that the righteousness of God is the demonstration and display of the power of God as the creative, forensic, and salvific work of God on behalf of his creation in the midst of history. This divine righteousness not only initiates a state of reconciliation with God, but leads to a reconciled life with and on behalf of others. Hence, both the present and the future must be evaluated eschatologically from the standpoint of the overlapping of the ages in which the kingdom of God is here, but not yet here in its fullness. Based on this apocalyptic worldview, Stuhlmacher's biblical theology, in the line of Augustine and Luther, is built upon a single, unified, comprehensive definition of the righteousness of God within the NT canon. In turn, and over against the overwhelming tide of contemporary scholarship, Stuhlmacher's continuing study has led him to contend for a unified theological development from the Old Testament to Jesus, and from Jesus to the early Church, and from the early Church to Paul and the other writings of the New Testament![43] Moreover, in contrast to the many contemporary voices who seek to relegate the theme of God's righteousness to a merely subsidiary concern within the New Testament, Stuhlmacher has continued to argue that the righteousness of God remains central both to the ministry of Jesus and to the Gospel of Paul and John, the methodological and exegetical foundation for which was already laid in his dissertation. Any evaluation of Stuhlmacher's program for doing biblical theology must therefore come to grips with this foundation, as well as with the subsequent historical and theological judgments which are built upon it as presented in the following essays.

NOTES

1. This essay is an expanded and adapted version of a paper first presented on January 18, 1992 as part of a seminar held by his students at the University of Tübingen in honor of Prof. Stuhlmacher's 60th. birthday entitled, " 'Gerechtigkeit Gottes' im Werk Peter Stuhlmachers. Eine Auseinandersetzung mit der eschatologischen Spannung zwischen imputativer und effektiver Gerechtigkeit im Neuen Testament."

2. Peter Stuhlmacher, *Gerechtigkeit Gottes bei Paulus*, FRLANT 87, 1966[2], p. 5. All translations of the German, where necessary, are my own. All citations throughout the work are given according to the original German versions unless otherwise explicitly indicated.

3. *Gerechtigkeit Gottes*, p. 5. In what follows, page references from Stuhlmacher's dissertation will be given in the body of the text.

4. Käsemann's essay "Gottesgerechtigkeit bei Paulus" was first published in *ZThK* 58 (1961) pp. 367-378) now also in his volume of collected essays, *Exegetische Versuche und Besinnungen*, BD. II, 1964 [1970[3]], pp. 181-193; Müller's was published as FRLANT 86, 1964. But as Stuhlmacher points out, this breakthrough first came in the short, but insightful essay by P. Kölbing, "Studien zur paulinischen

Theologie I, δικαιοσύνη θεοῦ in Röm 1,17," *ThStKr* 68 (1895) pp. 7-17. Kölbing argued that the righteousness of God in Rom 1:17 can be seen to refer to God's own activity once one realizes that the entire thought world of Paul was intimately interwoven with the early Christian eschatology and once one recognizes as well that the natural background for understanding the terminology of the righteousness of God in Paul is the Old Testament (p. 38). It was in Kölbing's combination of early Christian eschatology with an Old Testament and Jewish background that Stuhlmacher first saw exemplified the way back to recapturing Paul's thought. Against this backdrop Kölbing saw that the link in Rom 1:17 between the future eschatological righteousness of God as judge and the present demonstration of salvation is to be found in the apocalyptic conception that the future eschatological powers in heaven were already active in the present in order to prepare for their final revelation (p. 38, quoting Kölbing, "Studien," pp. 14f.). In view of Kölbing's programmatic, but unheeded contribution, and with the impetus of Käsemann's renewed emphasis on the apocalyptic nature of Paul's theology, Stuhlmacher's goal in his dissertation was to provide a comprehensive discussion of the Old Testament and Jewish backdrop to Paul's apocalyptic thought concerning the righteousness of God (cf. pp.102-184) and to extend the perspective outlined by Kölbing to all the relevant Pauline texts (pp.74-101). As a result, he sought to demonstrate what Kölbing had failed to do, namely to show "that on this basis the unity of the judicial and ethical conceptions of justification can be established and in doing so overcome their traditional antithesis" (p. 39).

5. Stuhlmacher's own conclusion concerning the meaning of the righteousness of God in Paul's thought followed the breakthrough of H. Cremer, who in 1900 had already interpreted Paul's thinking against the backdrop of the Old Testament. In doing so, he contended that "righteousness"(צדק[ה]) was a relational concept referring to the relationship between God and his people, so that God's righteousness is a "*iustitia salutifera* which, although judicial, works to bring about salvation; hence the Old Testament does not know a punitive righteousness of God" (p. 46, Stuhlmacher is referring to Cremer's work, *Die paulinische Rechtfertigungslehre im Zusammenhang ihrer geschichtlichen Voraussetzungen*, 1900², pp. 23, 33f., 51f.). Although Cremer's work remained isolated, Stuhlmacher's own study also demonstrated that the origin of Paul's use of the righteousness of God terminology was not the meaning of "righteousness" in Greek thought, in which "righteousness refers to conduct (of mankind and the gods) over against a standard of justice" (p.105). Nor was its origin to be found in Hellenistic Judaism, as illustrated by the differences between Paul on the one hand, and Philo and Josephus on the other (p. 107). Rather, the origin of Paul's thinking was clearly the Old Testament, even though the singular form צדקת יהוה is found in the Old Testament only in Deuteronomy

33:21 (p. 109), and this exact terminology never occurs in the LXX (p. 112). For Stuhlmacher observed that in the LXX, "the genitive formulation δικαιοσύνη τοῦ κυρίου (= "righteousness of the Lord") always designated God's own just conduct; the righteousness before or from God is designated, to put it precisely linguistically, diκαιοσύνη ἐνώπιον θεοῦ (Tob. 13:8) or ἡ παρὰ τοῦ θεοῦ δικαιοσύνη (Bar 5:2, 9)" (p. 112). Stuhlmacher thus concluded that, "on the basis of the feel for the language of Hellenistic Judaism as found in the Septuagint it would be entirely unmotivated to translate δικαιοσύνη in Paul's thought as 'righteousness from God' or 'righteousness before God' " (p. 112). Instead, Stuhlmacher's study led to the conclusion that within the Old Testament, the singular use of צדקת יהוה (= the "righteousness of YHWH") in Deut 33:21 represented the high degree of theological reflection which was signified by the many references to God's righteousness with other terminology and with the plural form צדקות יהוה (pp. 144f.). Hence, "if (in Deut 33:21) a singular is formed from the plural technical term, this means that, as a result, the streams of tradition that speak of Yahweh's faithfulness to the community as experienced in the cult and which alone creates salvation also come together in this concept" (p. 145). It was this tradition that was then picked up in the Jewish apocalyptic literature and tradition.

6. "Die Gerechtigkeitsanschauung des Apostels Paulus," in his *Versöhnung, Gesetz und Gerechtigkeit, Aufsätze zur biblischen Theologie*, 1981, pp. 87-116, p. 105n.16 (now as "The Apostle Paul's View of Righteousness," in his *Reconciliation, Law, & Righteousness, Essays in Biblical Theology*, 1986, pp. 68-93).

7. "Die Gerechtigkeitsanschauung des Apostels Paulus," pp. 106f.

8. Cf. "Die Gerechtigkeitsanschauung des Apostels Paulus," pp. 106f. and p. 106n.16.

9. *Paul's Letter to the Romans, A Commentary*, trans. Scott J. Hafemann, 1994, p. 30 (for the original, see *Der Brief an die Römer*, NTD 6, 1989, p. 31).

10. See e.g. the influential work of E.P. Sanders, *Paul and Palestinian Judaism, A Comparison of Patterns of Religion*, 1977, pp. 463ff.

11. "Die Gerechtigkeitsanschauung des Apostels Paulus," p. 93.

12. "Die Gerechtigkeitsanschauung des Apostels Paulus," p. 93.

13. Cf. the two new articles in his 1981 collection of essays, *Versöhnung, Gesetz und Gerechtigkeit*: "Die neue Gerechtigkeit in der Jesusverkündigung" and "Jesu Auferweckung und die Gerechtigkeitsanschauung der vorpaulinischen Missionsgemeinden," now translated as "The New Righteousness in the Proclamation of Jesus," and "Jesus' Resurrection and the View of Righteousness in the Pre-Pauline Mission

Congregations," in *Reconciliation, Law, & Righteousness, Essays in Biblical Theology*, pp. 30-49 and 50-67 respectively. For this key point, see his conclusion, "Jesu Auferweckung," p. 86.

14. See his pivotal article, "Existenzstellvertretung für die Vielen: Mk 10,45 (Mt 20,28)," originally published in *Werden und Wirken des Alten Testaments, FS C. Westermann zum 70. Geburtstag*, ed. R. Albertz, et. al., 1980, pp.412-427, now as "Vicariously Giving His Life for Many, Mark 10:45 (Matt 20:28)," in his *Reconciliation, Law, & Righteousness, Essays in Biblical Theology*, pp. 16-29.

15. "Jesusverkündigung," p. 45.

16. "Jesusverkündigung," p. 47

17. "Jesusverkündigung," p. 45, emphasis his. For an outline of Stuhlmacher's understanding of the person and work of Jesus, based on the centrality of his messianic self-understanding as expressed in Mark 10:45, see now his *Jesus of Nazareth, Christ of Faith*, 1994.

18. "Jesusverkündigung," p. 60. Stuhlmacher's understanding of Jesus' messianic self-understanding and of his corresponding commitment to go to the cross in view of this Old Testament background was then confirmed and supported by the work of his colleague H. Gese and Gese's student B. Janowski, cf. "Jesusverkündigung," p. 61, quoting Gese, "Die Sühne," in his *Zur biblischen Theologie*, 1977, pp. 85-106, p.104.

19. "Jesusverkündigung," p. 49.

20. "Jesusverkündigung," p. 49, emphasis his.

21. "Jesusverkündigung," p. 51.

22. Cf. "Gerechtigkeitsanschauung des Apostels Paulus," pp. 100, 102.

23. "Gerechtigkeitsanschauung des Apostels Paulus," p. 100.

24. Cf. "Gerechtigkeitsanschauung des Apostels Paulus," pp. 100-105.

25. "Gerechtigkeitsanschauung des Apostels Paulus," p. 101.

26. Cf. *Gerechtigkeit Gottes*, p. 85.

27. "Gerechtigkeitsanschauung des Apostels Paulus," p. 102.

28. "Jesusverkündigung," p .60.

29. "Gerechtigkeitsanschauung des Apostels Paulus," p. 101.

30. "Gerechtigkeitsanschauung des Apostels Paulus," p. 104.

31. "Gerechtigkeitsanschauung des Apostels Paulus," p. 104.

32. "Gerechtigkeitsanschauung des Apostels Paulus," p. 105.

33. "Gerechtigkeitsanschauung des Apostels Paulus" p. 105n. 16.

34. *Paul's Letter to the Romans*, p. 31; original: *Römerbrief*, pp. 31f.

35. Naturally, Stuhlmacher's readers will also have to decide whether or not they can accept his historical judgments concerning the reliability of the NT traditions (especially the Jesus traditions!), as well as his emphasis on the essential theological and salvation-historical

unity of the OT and NT, an evaluation of which is beyond the scope of this paper. Suffice it to say that this reader finds them convincing. Moreover, in regard to the material question concerning Stuhlmacher's interpretation of the meaning of the "righteousness of God" itself, see for a general orientation to the question, John Reumann, *Righteousness in the New Testament, "Justification" in the United States Lutheran - Roman Catholic Dialogue*, 1982, and now both for a summary of the debate and for his own contribution to the discussion, see especially Mark A. Seifrid, *Justification by Faith, The Origin and Development of a Central Pauline Theme*, Supplements to Novum Testamentum 68, 1992.

36. Cf. the experimental model which Stuhlmacher developed for the commentary series Evangelisch-Katholischer Kommentar zum Neuen Testament in his *Der Brief an Philemon*, EKK XVIII, 19812. The "experiment," in his words, was to attempt "to put forth a theological exegesis which reflected the history of interpretation and its effects," which could serve as a new model for the commentary genre (p. 7). This same approach was also applied to the presentation of Stuhlmacher's own hermeneutical program, see now his *Vom Verstehen des Neuen Testaments. Eine Hermeneutik*, NTD Ergänzungsreihe 6, 19862.

37. See *Gerechtigkeit Gottes*, pp. 11-73. Hence, for example, the driving force and significance of Karl Barth's work as a whole can be measured against his own analysis of the theological tradition he inherited as presented in his formative lectures of 1932-1933, now published in his 1946 work, *Die protestantische Theologie im 19. Jahrhundert* (now in English as *Protestant Theology in the Nineteenth Century*, 1959).

38. For Stuhlmacher's critique of the modern practice of historical-criticism and his own proposal for its reform, see in English his brief study, *Historical Criticism and Theological Interpretation of Scripture*, 1977, which is just one essay from his larger collected work, *Schriftauslegung auf dem Wege zur biblischen Theologie*, 1975, which together with his detailed study, *Vom Verstehen des Neuen Testaments*, provide the larger context of his critique as well as his own proposals.

39. Stuhlmacher's ongoing work on the righteousness of God can be seen to be a development of Luther's fundamental insight that the *iustitia dei* is God's work, which Stuhlmacher deems to be "Luther's real exegetical accomplishment" (p. 18). But as Stuhlmacher observed in his dissertation, Luther's understanding of the righteousness of God is consequently characterized by the fact that he interprets every reference to the righteousness of God as the righteousness of faith, thus consistently seeing them to be speaking of the gift of God (p. 19). Yet for Luther this emphasis on the gift of God was never separated from God's act as the giver, so that God's righteousness was inextricably linked to his creative activity as an expression of his grace, rather than primarily to a divine attribute (pp. 19n.7, 20). Unfortunately, due to

Luther's opposition to the tradition which he inherited, with its emphasis on the necessity of works before the future judgment of God and its optimistic anthropology, he himself emphasized clearly only the gift-character of the righteousness of God. The righteousness of God as God's own salvific rule was expressed only in Luther's early writings and was later easily overlooked by those who followed him (cf. pp. 23-24). As for Calvin, Stuhlmacher points out, p. 24, that he interpreted the righteousness of God both as a reference to the character of God as judge and to God's merciful faithfulness to his own promises and covenant in which God's righteousness is his power as creator (cf. *Inst.* II.8.19f.; 16.3; III.12.1.2; 18.7; 23.2, 4; 25.5). Nevertheless, in his interpretation of Romans, Calvin too followed Luther in emphasizing primarily the gift-character of the righteousness of God, though he moved from one pole to the other in his interpretation of Rom 1:17 and in 3:26 spoke of two ways in which the righteousness of God was revealed in Christ: as God's immeasurable righteousness *and* as its bestowal on mankind (pp. 24f.).

40. The extensive works of W. D. Davies' *Paul and Rabbinic Judaism*, 1980[4], H. J. Scheops' *Paul: The Theology of the Apostle in the Light of Jewish Religious History*, 1959, and P. Stuhlmacher's own *Das paulinische Evangelium*, 1968, showing that the most relevant conceptual backdrop to Paul's thinking is the Old Testament and post-biblical Judaism, were crucial in turning the tide. Hence, the observation of E.P. Sanders in 1977, *Paul and Palestinian Judaism*, p. 7, still remains true a 14 years later: "If it is not universally conceded that the most pertinent 'background' to study in order to understand Paul is Judaism, that position is at least clearly dominant."

41. *Gerechtigkeit Gottes*, p. 57, referring to Barth, KD IV, 1, pp. 591ff., 613.

42. *Gerechtigkeit Gottes*, pp. 57f., referring to Barth, *Römerbrief*, to 10:3.

43. As the following essays make clear, in taking this path Stuhlmacher's biblical theology is indebted to and part of a wider tradition of contemporary scholarship marked by the important works of scholars such as J. Jeremias, O. Cullmann, B. Gerhardsson, R. Riesner, H. Riesenfeld, H. Schürmann, Ben F. Meyer, B. Childs, L. Goppelt, Friedrich Mildenberger, and especially his Tübingen colleagues Hartmut Gese, Martin Hengel, Otto Betz, and Otfried Hofius.

1

THE PLANNING AND REALIZATION OF A BIBLICAL THEOLOGY[1]

A Biblical Theology of the New Testament which deserves this name must suit the biblical texts hermeneutically, i.e. it must attempt to interpret the Old and New Testament tradition as it wants to be interpreted.[2] For this reason, it cannot read these texts only from a critical distance as historical sources but must, at the same time, take them seriously as testimonies of faith which belong to the Holy Scripture of early Christianity. Accordingly, when drawing up a Biblical Theology of the Old or New Testament (or of both testaments at the same time), historical and dogmatic aspects will overlap. Furthermore, at issue is the difficult problem, which is still debated today, of how the Old and New Testaments relate to one another.

The Christian Bible has been made up of Old and New Testaments since the time of the ancient Church, and churches ever since have had good reason for their belief that the two-part canon bears witness to the triune God. Nevertheless, it has become standard procedure in exegetical scholarship to work with the Old and New Testaments separately and to discuss the question concerning the unity of both testaments in the one Christian canon only on special occasions. This development is as understandable as it is regrettable. It is understandable, because there exists a scholarly division of labor: historical scholarship and the theological penetration of the Old and New Testaments have become so complicated in the last 150 years that individual scholars are barely, if at all, able to command a view of all the biblical disciplines and are, therefore, unable to do scholarly work in the areas of both Old and New Testament. This development is regrettable, because it allows an awareness of the unity of the two testaments to die out and it encourages a perpetuation of the false impression that the Old and New Testaments were united into the one Christian canon only at a later date and could only be held together through the clamp of Christian doctrine. When one also considers that the Hebrew Bible, the so-called *Tanak*, which is made up of the Law, the Prophets and the Writings, was and is the Holy Scripture of Judaism, then one can be misled, beyond the false impression just mentioned, to the conclusion that the "Old Testament" (as the Christians came to call it) is the original and genuine Bible of Israel, while only the New Testament can be considered the Bible of the Christians. If things are viewed in this way, one can even begin to consider whether Israel was not deprived of her (Hebrew) Bible through the creation of the two-part Christian canon by the early Church. But as unfortunate as these false conclusions may be, there is no way to turn back the clock and do away with the division of biblical scholarship into the disciplines of Old and New Testament. If this is so, then one must at least vigorously insist that the two disciplines not lose sight of one another and not fail to perform their common theological task! Thus the time has come for Christian theology to reflect upon the fact *that the Old and New Testaments have belonged together in a most intimate way since the beginning of the Christian Church. They belong together to such a degree that the testimony of the New Testament cannot be adequately understood without the Old and the exegesis of the Old Testament remains incomplete without taking the New into view.*[3] Reflection upon this fact has been presented to my generation as an obligation by the Old and New Testament scholars LEONARD GOPPELT, GERHARD VON RAD, WALTHER ZIMMERLI, CLAUS WESTERMANN and HANS-WALTER WOLFF, as well as the dogmatic theologian KARL BARTH, and it is now time for it to be realized, no longer in the form of thoughts and theses only, but in a complete Biblical Theology of the Old and New Testaments.

1. *The necessity of the perspective of Biblical Theology*

If we take the New Testament as our starting point, there are four main factors which force us at the very outset of any historical and theological exegesis to take the Old Testament into account as well.

1.1 The first and most important factor is that Jesus of Nazareth and the apostles chosen by him, including Paul, who was called only after Easter, were all Jews by birth and thus gave Christianity, from the very beginning, a share in the Holy Scriptures of Israel. Jesus and the apostles first taught the Jewish men and women who believed their message and then later the Gentiles to read "the Holy Scripture(s)" (cf. for this term 2 Macc 8:23 and Rom 1:2) as the inspired word of the one God (cf. Deut 6:4) who created the world, chose Israel to be his own people, and sent his Son Jesus (of Nazareth) to redeem as Christ both Jews and Gentiles. *As far as Jesus and the apostles are concerned, "the Holy Scriptures" do not belong to Israel alone, but to all Jews and Gentiles who believe Jesus to be Lord and Christ.*

1.2 Second, the oldest literary version of the Christian confession which the New Testament has to offer us is the "gospel" which Paul cites in 1 Cor 15:3-5. This confession already understands the death and resurrection of Jesus the Messiah by means of "the Scriptures" *(*κατὰ τὰς γραφάς to be the quintessential salvation-event (or Heilsgeschehen), brought about by God. In addition, the old narrative summary of the gospel in Acts 10:36-43 depends on its continual reference to "the Scripture."[4] Both texts clearly show that *a correct Christian understanding of the person* *and mission of Jesus, as well as his passion and resurrection, was and is to be achieved only with the help of the testimony of "the Scriptures."*

1.3 The third factor to be considered concerns the text of the Holy Scripture itself and the books which it included. In the first century CE, they were read by the Jews and Christians in Hebrew, Aramaic, and Greek, and—despite the priority of the Hebrew over the Greek text—both text forms were considered to be inspired.[5] After the tradition had developed within Israel for many centuries, the Hebrew Bible, from the fourth century B.C. onward, became canonically fixed in three steps. The Torah was canonized first, in the second century BCE the Prophets followed, while the delimitation of the third part of the canon, containing the Writings, lasted till the end of the first century CE (and even longer).[6] The history of the formation of the Septuagint falls in this same time period. In the third century BCE, first the Pentateuch and then somewhat later the Prophets were translated into Greek; but the translation of the Writings was completed only gradually and lasted until the beginning of the second century CE. Since the translated Hebrew and Aramaic writings were supplemented with several edifying and instructional Judeo-Hellenistic books without Semitic original texts, (like, for example, the Wisdom of Solomon and Fourth Maccabees), the Septuagint had a larger size than did the Hebrew Bible. Although there was never an attempt from the Jewish side to finally canonize the Septuagint, it was of great importance for ancient Judaism and for early Christianity. The formulation of the New Testament testimony to Christ is unthinkable without it.[7] The New Testament and the apostolic fathers assume their readers know of and have read the Septuagint and cite its edifying writings as "Scripture" (γραφή), just as they do the Law, the Prophets and the Psalms (cf., for example, James 1:19 with Sir 5:11[Hebr.]; Mk 10:19 with Sir 4:1 [LXX]; Barn 19:2, 9 with Sir 7:30 [and 4:31]). Thus, as the fundamental New Testament traditions were being written down, the Hebrew Bible and the Septuagint were certainly recognized by Jews and Christians alike to be Holy Scripture, but both the Hebrew and the Greek canons were still open. *The New Testament books are not placed opposite an Old Testament which had long been fixed as to its contents; rather, they refer to a collection of "Holy Scriptures" written in Hebrew and Greek which are still canonically unclosed, and they testify to a continuity of God's activity in and through Christ, a continuity of salvation history* (cf. Luke 16:16 and Heb 1:1-2).

1.4 The fourth factor concerns the formation of the Christian biblical canon out of the Old and New Testaments. The question whether the Old Testament of the Christian Church should comprise only the books of the Hebrew Bible or embrace the inventory of writings from the Septuagint was discussed until the fourth Century CE (and is even today not completely answered). It is interesting to note that this discussion was almost always connected with the question of the extent of the New Testament and its relation to the Old. Therefore, in the most important witnesses to the Christian history of the canon, the books of the Old and New Testaments are listed together. Of course, scholars can describe the development of the Old Testament and genesis of the New Testament separately (for example in the so-called Introductions to the Old and New Testaments), but this description should not cause us to forget that the relation of the New Testament to the Old and the witnesses to the history of the canon testify to the intertwining of both processes. If, when considering the development of Old and New Testaments, one also pays due attention to history of the Septuagint, then it becomes absolutely necessary to speak of *only one complex canonical process* from which the Hebrew Bible, the Septuagint and the New Testament all emerged.

1.5 Taking all of these points together, we can make

two inferences which are of great importance for a Biblical Theology (of the Old and/or New Testament):

1.5.1 In the Christian churches, the individual traditions and books of the New Testament formed from the very beginning, together with the "Holy Scripture," the foundation for the two-part Christian canon.

1.5.2 The New Testament cannot be (and does not want to be) understood without the Old. It at no time attempts to replace the "Holy Scriptures." It only wants to testify to God's definitive revelatory act in and through his one and only Son Jesus. Part of this testimony is teaching about what faith in Jesus Christ means and how the "Holy Scriptures" are to be understood in relation to God's final act of salvation in this Christ.

2. *The Realization of the Perspective of Biblical Theology*

In order to pursue these theses further, we need to clarify in what way the New Testament relates back to the Old Testament and where the crucial points of reference with regard to content lie between the Old and New Testament Scriptures.

2.1 The relationship assumed to exist between the Old and New Testament today is the result of an inadmissible abstraction. Instead of focusing on the common canonical process from which the two Testaments emerged (see above), the Old and New Testaments are seen as two groups of writings which are independent of one another and which were only later brought together to form the canon of the Church. It is thus assumed that the Old Testament canon of the Law, the Prophets and the Writings was already closed in the second or first century BCE, and that the so-called Intertestamental Period began about 160 BCE, after which the books of the New Testament were written between 50 and 120 CE. Therefore, whoever desires to gain an historical understanding of the New Testament must first take note of the specific testimony of the Old Testament, then take time to become familiar with the Intertestamental Period, after that, study the New Testament, and then, in one last step, attempt to understand the construction of the two-part Christian canon and, at the same time, bring together the independent testimony of the Old and New Testaments in recognition of their dogmatic importance for the Church. The impressive work of BREVARD S. CHILDS, *Biblical Theology of the Old and New Testaments*, 1992, is constructed according to this method,

If one is to go beyond this abstraction, one must (with CHILDS) pay more attention to the canonical process which produced the Old and New Testaments, but must also include the development and influence of the Septuagint to a much higher degree than is usually the case (and as is the case with CHILDS). If this is done, it is no longer possible to speak of a long Intertestamental Period. But if this period of division never existed, then it is impossible to divide the New Testament sharply from the Old with respect to content and to time. One therefore does well to realize and take into consideration not only that ancient Judaism produced the Hebrew Bible and the Septuagint, but also that Judaism deserves to be given special attention when studying the New Testament![8] Since Jesus and the authors of the New Testament were Jews (see above) and the majority of Christians in the first century were mainly recruited from the vicinity of the synagogue (of the Diaspora), Judaism was for all of them in no way simply a phenomenon (among others) of their religio-historical "environment," but was the religious context within which and for which they developed their message. The authors of the New Testament and those for whom they wrote lived in the Jewish faith, and for them the Tanak and the Septuagint were "Holy Scripture" which they learned and through which they heard the voice of the living God (as the Father of Jesus Christ).[9] In formulating their gospel message and

Christian teachings, the New Testament witnesses did not simply conform to the linguistic and religious needs of the Hellenistic Period; rather, they formulated the testimony to Christ in close adherence to the inspired Holy Scriptures and the Jewish tradition of faith. It was only this special formulation of these testimonies which kept the New Testament traditions from sinking into oblivion as did other religious works of the Hellenistic Period.

2.3 Second, if progress is to be made over against the usual schematic conception of the relation of the New Testament to the Old mentioned above, then the references of the New Testament to the Old must be comprehensively taken into account, and not just partially.

2.3.1 Every reader of the New Testament notices the many *direct quotations* from the Old Testament which riddle the four Gospels, the letters of Paul, the Letter to the Hebrews and, for example, also 1 Peter. Most of these quotations come from the Law, the Prophets and the Psalms. Examples are superfluous.

2.3.2 A careful reading of the New Testament also reveals an abundance of allusions to texts and events from the Old Testament. Today, these are harder to verify than are the direct quotations; they were easier to understand within the context of early Judaism and early Christianity because the Holy Scripture was generally well known in the early Christian churches. Some good examples of these are Jesus writing in the sand (John 8:6, 8, cf. with Jer 17:13), Jesus' characteristic association of forgiveness of sins with healing (Mark 2,10-11 par., cf. with Ps 103:3), or his final cry on the cross according to John 19:30: "It is finished" (cf. with Gen 2:1-2).

2.3.3 A third observation to be made is that, alongside the quotations and allusions, the New Testament is related to the Old through a common tradition *of language and life experience*. This is manifested in a common mode of expression and in common concepts. Some of the many examples are: the creation doctrine which is common to both the Old and the New Testaments, the common idea of the "kingdom of God" (βασιλεία τοῦ θεοῦ), which is soon to come, the concept of God "dwelling" upon the earth, the belief that there exists a direct relation between the deeds of a person and his or her condition, and the expectation of a resurrection of the dead at the end of time. If one pays due attention to all of these common possessions, it becomes difficult to continue to dispute that even those books in the New Testament which do not directly cite the Old Testament—for example Colossians and the letters of John—have a connection with the "Holy Scriptures."

This threefold, relationship which the New Testament has with the Old would also suggest that in drawing up a Biblical Theology of the New Testament one needs to be concerned not only with Old Testament quotes and allusions,[10] but also to take fully into consideration the complex traditio-historical relationship of the testaments one to another. In attempting to do this, one must be continually aware of the fact *that the New Testament books want to be read only in addition to the "Holy Scriptures" as testimonies to the conclusive revelation of God in and through Jesus Christ.*

2.4 There are many places where the New Testament relates to the Old with regard to its contents. *The reigning center of these points of reference is the New Testament testimony to Christ.* At the beginning of the first volume of his *Theologie des Neuen Testaments* [published posthumously in 1975 by JÜRGEN ROLOFF], LEONHARD GOPPELT put it very well in noting: "For the way in which the New Testament viewed itself, it is, in our opinion,—despite all variations in the individual writings—fundamental that it intends to witness to an event of fulfillment which comes from God and which proceeds from Jesus at its center."[11]

When one examines this principle, one is continually confronted with facts and statements which connect the New Testament with the Old. The most important are as follows:

2.4.1 In the Lord's Prayer, Jesus taught his disciples to call upon the one God (from Deut 6:4) and that his name—i.e the name JHWH!—be hallowed (Matt 6:9; Luke 11:21). Jesus understood himself to be the "Son" of this God (cf. Matt 11:25; Luke 10:21) and (meaning the same thing) the messianic Son of God (cf. Mark 8:27-33, 38 par.; 14:61-62 par.). His (Jewish) disciples accepted this claim of authority, while his (Jewish) enemies rejected it and condemned Jesus to die as a blasphemer of God.

2.4.2 From Easter on, Jesus' person, his mission, his death on the cross, his resurrection and his future work were interpreted by the early Christians with the help of the Holy Scriptures (cf. 1 Cor 15:3-5, 20-28; Luke 24:25-27; John 2:22; 12:16; 20:9; Acts 10:34-43). Also, *all* of the New Testament titles for Jesus (Christ, Son of God, Son of Man, Servant of God, Lamb of God, Lord, Savior, Word, etc.) have an Old Testament-Jewish origin!

2.4.3 Also, the way the New Testament spoke of God is characterized by a combination of Old Testament-Jewish and early Christian beliefs. A classic example of this development of Christian confessions of faith out of Old Testament-Jewish traditions can be seen in Rom 4. According to Rom 4:5, God justifies the wicked (ἁμαρτωλούς) who believe in him; according to Rom 4:17, he is the creator who calls that which does not exist into existence and makes the dead come alive (cf. 2 Bar [syr] 48 and the second of the Eighteen Benedictions[12]) and in Rom 4:24-25 he is called the one God who delivered Jesus our Lord over to death for our sins and raised him to life for our justification (cf. with Isa 53:11-12).[13]

The center of the New Testament, the gospel of Jesus Christ, is thoroughly formulated in Old Testament language and bears witness to the eschatological salvation provided by God for Jews and Gentiles. This testimony connects the New Testament inextricably with the Old. Because of this Christological clamp, the Old Testament belongs to Jews and Christians alike, and the gospel of God concerning Jesus Christ is intended "first for the Jew, then for the Gentile" (Rom 1:16). It invites us all to join in the confession that Jesus is the Lord whom God raised from the dead (Rom 10:9-10), since eschatological salvation for Jews and Gentiles alike depends on this confession.

The *fundamental* correlation between Old and New Testaments, which has become clearly evident, has, furthermore, consequences for the conception and composition of a Biblical Theology of the New Testament.

3. *The realization of a Biblical Theology of the New Testament*

According to Karl Barth, Theology as a whole has—as Ernst Fuchs so nicely put it "*been given the honor to join with God on his path to humanity and to gather up people upon this path.*"[14] This insight also directs a Biblical Theology of the New Testament in the way it should go and, at the same time, emphasizes a point about methodology which was mentioned at the beginning. If it is really the task of a theological exegesis of the Bible to demonstrate God's path to humanity in and through Jesus Christ and also to gather up people upon this path, then both historical and dogmatic argumentation overlap in the the field of Biblical Theology of the Old and New Testament, and this is due to the very nature of the task at hand.

To be more specific, a Biblical Theology of the New Testament which desires to do justice to the testimony of the texts must elucidate four things. First, it must be shown that the New Testament message of faith comes thoroughly from the Old Testament and that the Old Testament testimonies pointed forward to the events of fulfillment in the New Testament. Second, it must be set forth that God, through the mission, passion, and resurrection of Jesus, provided salvation for Jews and Gentiles at a time when both were still godless and unbelieving sinners (Rom 5:6, 8). Third, the historical development and diversity othe post-Easter testimony to Christ and to the faith must be traced and explained. Fourth and finally, it must be shown how the Old and New Testaments came together to form the two-part Christian canon, where the theological center of this canon lies, and what hermeneutical demands it places upon theological exegesis.

> I have proposed in my book, *Biblische Theologie des Neuen Testaments* 1 (1992) p. 13,[15] a concrete outline for a Biblical Theology of the New Testament which meets the criteria just mentioned. After a discussion of principal questions of exegesis and hermeneutics, a first, major section deals with the origin and character of the preaching of the New Testament, and, in a second major section, the origin of the two-part Christian canon, the question of "the center of Scripture," and the problem of biblical hermeneutics are discussed.

In the following, only three complexes can be selected from the whole scope of problems mentioned: the preaching ministry of Christ and the beginnings of Christology, the testimony of Paul and the school of John, and the twofold question about the "center" of the Bible and its proper interpretation.

NOTES

1. In all of my efforts concerning Biblical Theology, I have thankfully profited from years of sustained dialogue with my friends E. EARLE ELLIS, HARTMUT GESE, MARTIN HENGEL, OTFRIED

HOFIUS, ULRICH MAUSER, ROBERT GUELICH (†) and FRIEDRICH MILDENBERGER and from communication with colleagues working in Biblical Theology in Old and and New Testament Studies, as well as those in the field of Dogmatics: OSWALD BAYER, BREVARD S. CHILDS, KLAUS HAACKER, TRAUGOTT HOLTZ, HANS HÜBNER, BERND JANOWSKI, GISELA KITTEL, KLAUS KOCH, HELMUT MERKLEIN, BEN F. MEYER, HANS-PETER RÜGER (†) HANS HEINRICH SCHMID, HORST SEEBASS and MICHAEL WELKER.

2. Cf. H Gese, "Hermeneutische Grundsätze der Exegese biblischer Texte," in his *Alttestamentliche Studien*, 1991, pp. 249-265 (esp. p. 249).

3. Cf H. Gese, "Erwägungen zur Einheit der biblischen Theologie," in his *Vom Sinai zum Zion*, 1974, pp. 11-30. B. S. CHILDS has long criticized GESE for inadmissibly constructing a traditio-historical trajectory which unifies Old and New Testaments, thus turning the Old Testament into "a historical object of the past," instead of emphasizing its "continuing role" in the canon as an "independent witness" (so recently in the German article B. S. CHILDS, "Biblische Theologie und christlicher Kanon," *JBTH* 3 [1988] 13-27 [esp. 24]). GESE responds to these (in my opinion totally unwarranted) criticisms in his article " Der auszulegende Text," in his *Alttestamentliche Studien* (see n. 2), pp. 266-282.

4. Cf. G. N. STANTON, *Jesus of Nazareth in New Testament Preaching*, 1974, p. 70f.

5. Cf. R. HANHART, "Die Bedeutung der Septuaginta in neutestamentlicher Zeit," *ZThK* 81 (1984) 395-416 (esp. 397ff.)

6. I thus follow the dating proposed by H. GESE, "Die dreifache Gestaltwerdung des Alten Testaments" in his *Alttestamentliche Studien* (see n. 2), pp. 1-28, and H. P. RÜGER, "Das Werden des christlichen Alten Testaments," *JBTh* 3 (1988) 175-189.

7. For the development of the Septuagint cf. R. HANHART, "Septuaginta," in W. H. SCHMIDT, W. THIEL, R. HANHART, *Altes Testament*, 1989, pp. 176-196, and M. HENGEL, "Die Septuaginta als von den Christen beanspruchte Schriftensammlung bei Justin und den Vätern vor Origenes," in *Jews and Christians*, (ed.) J. D. G. DUNN, 1992, pp. 39-84, as well as M. HENGEL (in collaboration with R. DEINES), "Die Septuaginta als 'christliche Schriftensammlung' und das Problem ihres Kanons," in *Verbindliches Zeugnis 1: Kanon—Schrift—Tradition*, (eds.) W. PANNENBERG and T. SCHNEIDER, Dialog der Kirchen, vol. 7,1992, pp. 24-127.

8. K. BERGER, *Exegese des Neuen Testaments*, 1977, p. 190, is fully justified in pointing this out.

9. For this cf. H. HÜBNER's nicely done monograph, *Gottes Ich und Israel*, 1984 and R. B. HAYS, *Echoes of Scripture in the Letters of Paul*, 1989, pp. 154-192.

10. As attempted by Hans Hübner, *Biblische Theologie des Neuen Testaments*, vol. 1, 1990; vol. 2, 1993. The third volume is forthcoming.

11. P. 50.

12. The 2nd benediction reads as follows (according to the translation appearing in E. FERGUSON, *Backgrounds of Early Christianity*, 1987, p. 459): "Thou art mighty, who bringest low the proud, strong, and He that judgeth the ruthless, that liveth for ever, that raiseth the dead, that maketh the wind to blow, that sendeth down the dew; that sustaineth the living, that quickeneth the dead; in the twinkling of an eye Thou makest salvation to spring forth for us. Blessed art Thou, O Lord, who quickenest the dead!"

13. For the significance of this observation for Biblical Theology, cf. P. STUHLMACHER, "Das Bekenntnis zur Auferweckung Jesu von den Toten und die Biblische Theologie" in my *Schriftauslegung auf dem Wege zur biblischen Theologie*, 1975, pp. 128-166.

14. Quoted from Hermann Diem, *Ja oder Nein*,1974, 290.

15. The second volume is forthcoming.

2

THE PREACHING OF JESUS AND NEW TESTAMENT CHRISTOLOGY

Just where a Biblical Theology of the New Testament is to begin is a subject of controversy. Should it begin with a description of Jesus' preaching, with the Easter message, or with the theology of Paul? One begins with Paul when one especially desires to take into account that the letters of Paul are the oldest New Testament writings that we have. The starting point is the Easter message when it is to be shown that all construction of tradition occurring in the New Testament is indebted above all to the events of Easter. The beginning is made with the preaching of Jesus when the goal is to trace the path which God took when he, in and through Jesus Christ, came to humanity.

1. *The preaching of Jesus as the starting point*

Beginning with the preaching of Jesus appears to me to be the most appropriate option from the standpoint of constructing a Biblical Theology for several reasons:

1.1 It is indeed true that the New Testament construction of tradition and the early Christian missionary testimony were first made possible by the experience of and the understanding provided by the resurrection of Jesus from the dead (cf., for example, Mark 9:9 par. John 14:26; Matt 28:16-20). Nevertheless, as the catechetical summary of the "gospel" in 1 Cor 15:3-5, the double-name Ἰησοῦς Χριστός, which developed out of the Jewish-Christian confession: "Jesus is the Messiah!" (without a predicate in the Semitic), the (pre-Lucan) preaching pattern in Acts 10:36-43, and Paul all indicate the gospel of God about Jesus Christ was not founded on human understanding, but by God's act of salvation in and through Jesus in history, which preceded all faith. "God demonstrates his own love for us in this: While we were still sinners, Christ died for us" (Rom 5:8). If the indications provided by the Bible are followed, then a Biblical Theology of the New Testament takes the preaching of Jesus as its starting point in order to demonstrate the *historical priority of God's act of salvation in and through Jesus over faith in Jesus Christ (which first began with Easter).*

1.2 Historical reasons also commend this starting point: Jesus was a Jew and lived in Palestine. His Jewish disciples and his prophetic "teacher" John the Baptist were interested in whether he was the promised Messiah (cf. Luke 7:18-23 par.; Mark 8:27-30 par.). He was then condemned to death by his Jewish enemies for being a pseudo-messianic blasphemer (cf. Mark 14:60-64 par.; 15:15, 26 par.). Thus, Jesus acted for and among people who were deeply formed by the early Jewish faith tradition. They were asking themselves whether Jesus' claim and his deeds were in concert with the Torah and the promises of the Prophets; a (very) few of them said that they were, while others said they were not and pressured the Roman prefect Pilate to have him crucified on the cross. These historical factors give the gospel of Jesus Christ its own unique historical contours, and, in order to preserve them, we make the preaching of Jesus the starting point for a Biblical Theology of the New Testament.

2. *Problems with the description*

If a Biblical Theology is begun with a description of

the preaching of Jesus, one must be careful to avoid three possible errors:

2.1 The first error takes place when individual scholars reconstruct the preaching of Jesus by autonomously choosing and arbitrarily arranging the sources. The main sources for understanding Jesus remain the four Gospels of the Bible. The apocryphal Gospels from the second century offer only secondary enlargements on and additions to the Gospel tradition.[1] Reports about Jesus of Nazareth outside the Bible are very sparse and should be used only with great care. It is obvious that in a Biblical Theology of the New Testament the Gospels must be the basis for any description, and one should only depart from their description when weighty historical or theological reasons exist for doing so.

2.2 The second error is to take a reconstructed picture of the so-called "historical Jesus," which is put together using scientific methods (and is thus hypothetical), and make it the theological norm by which the testimony of the Gospels is to be measured, or to identify without further examination this critical reconstruction with the testimony of the Gospels regarding Jesus' life and work. When working out a Biblical Theology of the New Testament, one must differentiate between the "historical" Jesus and the biblical testimony to Jesus Christ and their differences must be settled theologically. *According to the testimony of the Gospels (and the apostolic letters), Jesus is only understood correctly when he is understood on the basis of his divine mission, his passion, and his resurrection.*

2.3 The third error would be to consider the testimony of the Synoptic Gospels concerning the historically unique work of Jesus to be Christologically less significant than that of the Gospel of John or the apostolic letters. This attitude fails to recognize that it is these very Synoptic Gospels which invite us to think of God's work of salvation in and through Christ in a historically concrete way and to avoid reflecting upon this work of God only in dogmatic abstractions.

3. *The way of the Gospel tradition*

The main source of our knowledge of Jesus Christ is the Gospels. Therefore, a reconstruction of Jesus' work will depend on the question of how the tradition in the Gospels is to be judged.

3.1 Turning first to the synoptic material, the following views vie for acceptance in the present discussion:

3.1.1 Following the results of classical form criticism and redaction criticism, which have been worked out in the last 70 years by such scholars as RUDOLPH BULTMANN,[2] and MARTIN DIBELIUS,[3] most exegetes judge the synoptic tradition very critically. Only few logia, parables and miracle stories are attributed to Jesus himself. The main part of the material can be traced back only to the creative imaginations of the post-Easter Church and the teachings of early Christian prophets, who taught in the name of (the exalted) Jesus.[4]

3.1.2 The attempts of JOACHIM JEREMIAS[5] and MATTHEW BLACK[6] to modify this picture of the tradition with the help of a philologically exact working out of the Aramaic mother tongue of Jesus has enjoyed only partial success. Also, a new view of (synoptic) tradition which for 35 years has been successively developed by E. EARLE ELLIS,[7] BIRGER GERHARDSSON,[8] MARTIN HENGEL,[9] BEN F. MEYER,[10] HARALD RIESENFELD,[11] RAINER RIESNER[12] and HEINZ SCHÜRMANN[13] has generally fallen on deaf ears. According to these scholars, the decisive beginning of the synoptic (logia) tradition goes back to Jesus on earth. As the "messianic teacher of wisdom" (M. HENGEL), he instructed his disciples (μαθη–

ταί= pupils!) in his teachings, sent them out as missionaries, and told them (privately) about his own mission of messianic suffering. Since the women and men from the "school of Jesus" formed the core of the church in Jerusalem right after Easter (cf. Acts 1:13-14), there exists not only an impressive continuity with regard to individuals between the early Church and the pre-Easter circle of disciples, but also a continuity, which this circle carefully fostered, between the pre-Easter teachings of Jesus and the post-Easter "teaching of the apostles" (Acts 2,42) concerning Jesus Christ as they are assembled, above all, in the Synoptic Gospels. Because this view of the development of the Jesus tradition is capable of operating with fewer hypotheses than classical form-criticism and, furthermore, fits much better than it within the borders of early Jewish tradition, it is to be preferred to the usual critical view. Hence, we should *assume that the synoptic tradition is to be considered secondary only in those cases where the words of Jesus or narratives about him are formulated or accentuated in a way which is clearly post-Easter in its orientation.*[14]

3.2 Differing opinions also exist as to the historical quality and development of the Johannine Gospel traditions. But, although this is true, a certain consensus has been reached: their language and contents bear a stamp which they received only after Easter in the Johannine school. Thus, the synoptic tradition has priority before the Johannine in a reconstruction of the pre-Easter preaching of Jesus.

4. *The person, message and way of Jesus*

If the core material of the synoptic tradition stems from a continuity in teaching which can be traced back to Jesus himself, then the picture of Jesus painted by this tradition must be more understandable historically and more illuminating Christologically than the models of modern Gospel criticism, which assume that most Gospel tradition is post-Easter construction. Indeed, there is much to support this.

4.1 The Gospel of Mark begins with the obviously post-Easter words: The beginning of the gospel about Jesus Christ, the Son of God (Mark 1:1). Although the designation of Jesus as the Son of God (υἱὸς θεοῦ) in Mark 1:1 (and, for example, Rom 1:3-4; Acts 8:37; 1 John 4:15; Rev 2:18; etc.) has the character of a post-Easter confession, it expresses exactly who Jesus was on earth. This can be demonstrated by pointing to three synoptic findings.

4.1.1.To address God with the Aramaic (ἀββᾶ, Greek: πάτερ), which is expressly done in Mark 14:36 and is to be assumed in Luke 10:21 par., is, within the context of the early Jewish (prayer) tradition, strikingly direct, even if not singular. *It points to a nearness of Jesus to God which Jesus himself refers to as a father-son relationship* (cf. Luke 10:22 par.). According to Luke 11:2, Jesus allows all who pray the Lord's Prayer to participate in his own nearness to God. The post-Easter Church, therefore, had good reason to form out of Jesus' ἀββᾶ a liturgical call to God in the spirit of Jesus; Paul cites it in Gal 4:6 and Rom 8:15.

4.1.2. According to the reports in all three Synoptic Gospels, Jesus in Capernaum claimed the right for himself to forgive sins and to heal as God himself does (cf. Mark 2:10-11 par. with Ps 103:3). This claim resulted already here at the beginning of his ministry in Galilee in the charge of blasphemy (cf. Mark 2:7 par.). Both the Abba-tradition and Jesus' acting in divine authority document his sonship.

4.1.3 Pointing in the same direction is the question of John the Baptist in Luke 7:18-23 par., whether Jesus is the promised "one who was to come" (ὁ ἐρχόμενος) or whether John and his disciples should expect another (Messianic savior). Recently, a new, clearly pre-Christian fragment (4Q521) was identified among the texts from cave four of the Qumran. In the 13th line we read about the Messiah expected in the last days that, "Then he will heal the sick, bring the dead to life, preach the good news to the poor..."(cf. Isa 61:1).[15] In view of this text, there is no longer any justification for considering the question of the Baptist to be a construction of the post-Easter Church. On the contrary, it bears witness to a very interesting tension between Jesus and the Baptist and documents that Jesus is conscious of his *messianic* mission. He is the "one who is to come" in person, who drives out demons with the "finger of God" (cf. Luke 11:20) and preaches to the "poor" the liberating news of the kingdom of God (cf. Luke 4:16-21; 7,22 par. with Isa 61:1-2). Because he makes the dead to live as God himself does, *he is the Son, in whom humanity meets God himself.*[16]

4.2 This pericope about the Baptist already touches upon the basic question which proved (and proves) to be decisive not only for Jesus' life but also for the relationship between Jews and Christians: *Is Jesus the Messiah promised by the prophets or not?* According to Mark 14:61-62 par., Jesus was asked this question by the high priest, Caiaphas. The verses run as follows:

> 61 ...Again the high priest asked him, "Are you the Christ, the Son of the Blessed?"
> 62 And Jesus said, "I am; and you will see the Son of man sitting at the right hand of power; and coming with the clouds of heaven."[17]

This answer resulted in Jesus receiving the death penalty for blasphemy. Ever since then this confession (Ἰησοῦς Χριστός) has been the point of division. Today, many try to escape the significance and great historical burden which weighs upon this confession by claiming that the designation of Jesus as Χριστός is a product of the confessional insight and belief of the early Church, and by declaring the whole synoptic passion-story to be a secondary Christian construction. In doing this, they often resort to the historical argument that Jesus was not condemned to death on the cross by the Jews but by the Roman, Pilate.

Since a Biblical Theology of the New Testament is interested in the truth of God's work for humanity, we cannot be satisfied with such evasive answers but must persist with a more exact inquiry.

4.2.1 According to the view of the synoptic tradition which we favor, the events of the passion are, for the most part, authentically described in Mark. Also, according to this view, Jesus' confession regarding the Messiah before Easter is what led to the Christian confession "Jesus is the Messiah!" after Easter. The following reasons can be given in support of this view.[18]

4.2.1.1 As MARTIN HENGEL has shown on various occasions, it is the Messiah-question which holds the passion narrative together historically.[19] If one declares this question a later Christian construction, the events of the passion can no longer be historically explained. Also, although it is still often championed, the opinion that the whole of the Jewish trial against Jesus described by the Gospels is secondary because it contradicts the codified law of the Mishnah must be corrected. After JOSEF BLINZLER[20] and OTTO BETZ[21] had raised serious objections to this view, AUGUST STROBEL showed in his book, *Die Stunde der Wahrheit* (1980), that the hurried, nightly trial of Jesus was thoroughly in agreement with the law code of the Tosefta and Mishnah, the charge being that Jesus was a false prophet and a pseudo-messianic "seducer," (Greek: πλάνος Hebr.: מדיח or מסית) so that Israel must be protected from his machinations at all costs (cf. Deut 13:2-12; 17:12-13;18:20-22). That Strobel is on the right historical track is borne out by the fact that the Jewish accusation that Jesus was a "seducer" is indeed mentioned and discussed in Matt 27:63-64; John 7:12; Justin, Dial 69:7;108:2. If we add to these ponderings the fact, which has long been shown by NIELS ALSTRUP DAHL,[22] that the title on the cross (Mark 15:26 par.) is not a Christian formulation, but a

Roman one, and represents a historically dependable element in the tradition, then we have every reason to take the historical character of the synoptic passion narrative seriously: After unmasking him as a "seducer," the Jewish leaders, who could not themselves put someone to death (John 18:31), took Jesus before the Roman prefect and accused him of being a (pseudo) messiah. Pilate finally had Jesus crucified because he found Jesus' claim to be king over the Jewish people to be politically dangerous (cf Mark 15:2 par.).

4.2.1.2 The passion-story circles elliptically around two main points. The first is Jesus' determination to bring his mission to a decisive end in Jerusalem and to provide with his own life—should God require it (cf. Mark 14:36)—substitutionary atonement for Israel, and the second is his "good confession" (cf. 1 Tim 6:13) before Caiaphas and Pilate.

4.2.1.2.1 Jesus' determination to bring his mission to a decisive end in Jerusalem can be recognized in the fact that he made his way up to Jerusalem despite all warnings (cf. Mark 8:32 par.; Luke 13:31-33) and that, once there, he gave the powerful priesthood, through the so-called cleansing of the temple (Mark 11:15-17), the option either to ignore him and continue providing their cultic service, or to follow his call to repentance and to prepare for the temple in the kingdom of God, which is not made from human hands, and the cult which is appropriate to it. If the priests were not willing to respond to his call to decision, then Jesus was prepared to take the place of their useless sin-offerings for Israel[23] and to give his life as a ransom for Israel.[24] Also testifying to Jesus' willingness to suffer are the words with which he opens the farewell paschal-supper (Mark 14:22,24 par.). In both instances, Jesus interprets his path of suffering by using Isa 43:3-4 and 53:10-12: *He saw himself called, as the Messianic suffering servant, to suffer death for Israel.*

4.2.1.2.2 AUGUST STROBEL, in the book just mentioned, defends the position that the confession of Jesus before Caiaphas in Mark 14:61-62 has been described by the tradition in Mark in a way which is "highly appropriate."[25] One can confidently agree with this, since the question of the priest and the answer of Jesus are completely Semitic in their formulation and are congruent with Jesus' habit of connecting the Messiah-tradition and the Son of Man-tradition with respect to his own person (cf. just Mark 8:29-33 par.). The claim expressed by Jesus, that he was the returning Son of Man and judge of the world, in accordance with Dan 7:13, before whom the highest Jewish judges would have to give account of themselves, gave Caiaphas clear legal justification to speak of blasphemy and to speak out for the death of Jesus. Here was a man from Galilee who actually presumed to possess God's authority to judge in the end times. *In Mark, therefore, we are truly confronted with a sketchy, but historically authentic passion narrative.* In order to comprehend its theological meaning, we must now turn to the Easter events.

5. *The Easter events and the origin of Christology*

Whoever asks today about the origin of the Christian confession of Jesus as the Messiah, Savior and Lord, generally receives the reply that this confession first came into being through the events of Easter. This reply is correct insofar as the Easter events are literally of fundamental importance for the New Testament. But, at the same time, it is a distortion because it obscures the importance of the teaching, person and fate of Jesus for Christology.

5.1 The Easter events also have their undeniable historical dimension. They are perceivable in the archaeological finds related to the tomb of Christ, which can be seen in the Church of the Sepulcher in Jerusalem. These finds make it almost impossible to dismiss the tradition of the empty grave as a late apologetic legend of the Christian

Church.[26] But even more important is the realization that *only the Easter appearances of Jesus to the witnesses listed in 1 Cor 15:5-8 caused the formulation of the New Testament confessions and traditions.* Those who experienced an appearance of Christ, who encountered them with a heavenly light of glory from heaven, recognized in him the crucified Jesus, but, at the same time, learned to see in him the bodily resurrected "Son of God in power," who had been exalted to the right hand of God (Rom 1:4). They saw that he, beyond the abyss of his death and their own failure, had "re-accepted" and called them to faith in him (cf. Luke 15:1-2; Rom 15:7). This calling through the risen Christ gave them new courage to establish the first congregation of Jesus Christ in Jerusalem and to proclaim the exalted Christ as Savior of the last days, Lord and judge of Jews and Gentiles. But the appearances of Jesus could engender this effect and the early Christian confession of the resurrection and exaltation of Jesus could take on its characteristic style of language (cf. 1 Cor 15:3-5; Acts 2:36 and Rom 10:9) only because the witnesses lived in the Old Testament-Jewish expectation of the resurrection (cf. Isa 26:19; Dan 12:2-3; 2 Macc 7:9 and the second of the Eighteen Benedictions: "Blessed art Thou, O Lord, who quickenest the dead"), and knew of the promise in the Holy Scriptures that the Messiah (cf. 2 Sam 7:12-14; Ps 89:27-28; Ps 110:1; 118:17, 22) and the Servant of God (cf. Isa 49:6; 52:13-53:12) would be glorified and be appointed ruler. Also present in the minds of these "pupils of Jesus" was Jesus' own expectations of resurrection and exaltation (cf. Luke 12:8-9 par.; Mark 12:18-27 par.; 14:25-62 par.). It is therefore no historical accident that all early Christian confessions, beginning with 1 Cor 15:2, are in continuity with Old Testament-early Jewish tradition and with the teachings of Jesus.

5.2 In view of the revolutionary recognition that God had raised the crucified Jesus from the dead and "made this Jesus. . . both Lord and Christ" (Acts 2:36), it became, beginning with Easter, necessary to hold fast to the teachings of Jesus and the memory of his fate, as well as to develop a language of faith which enabled the young Church to praise God and the risen Lord and to do missionary work among the Jews and the Gentiles. The Gospels and the apostolic letters, the Acts of the Apostles and the Revelation of John, all gathered together in the one New Testament, are a result of this impulse stemming from Easter to create an independent faith tradition. Based on this impulse, it was merely a matter of logical development which led to the fact that all of these books which were read in the worship services of the Christian churches were gradually joined with the Holy Scriptures, and finally formed, together with them, the two-part Christian canon.

5.3 The central part of this New Testament formation of tradition is represented by *their Christological statements*. One recognizes, when looking at them, that they are not formulated simply from a post-Easter perspective, but that they are also indebted to the teachings of Jesus and the inspired word of God in the Holy Scriptures. They usually exhibit the following structure: *Through the insight provided by the Holy Spirit (cf. 1 Cor 2:10,16; John 14:26), the person, the way of suffering, or the work of the exalted Christ are described with the inspired words of the Holy Scriptures in such a way that it corresponds to the teachings of Christ and God's will to save (also testified to in the Holy Scriptures).*

5.3.1 This structure can be seen particularly well in Rom 4:25. Paul speaks in Rom 4:24 of faith in the God "who raised Jesus our Lord from the dead" and in 4:25 he adds a Christological formula in (synthetic) parallelismus membrorum: "He was delivered over to death for our sins and was raised to life for our justification." The two passives, παρεδόθη and ἠγέρθη, indicate (in a typically Jewish-Christian fashion) God's actions toward Jesus. This is done with reference to (the Hebrew text of) Isa 53:6,10-12 and in agreement with Jesus' own interpretation of his passion (see p. 23): God appointed Jesus to be the Servant of God and delivered him over to death in order that "our" sinful guilt might be eradicated, and raised him in order that "our" justification be achieved. Thus, "our" sins are atoned for through the atoning death of Jesus and through his resurrection "we" are justified; and this is done so that Jesus' atoning death will be effective "for us" in the last judgment and the risen Christ will intercede "for us" before God's judgment throne (cf. Rom 8:33-34 with Isa 53:12).

5.3.2 Not only Rom 4:25 bears witness to this threefold Christological structure, but also the short, two-word confessions: "Jesus is the Messiah" (Ἰησοῦς Χριστός) and "Jesus is Lord" (Κύριος Ἰησοῦς), as well as the summary of the gospel from 1 Cor 15:3b-5, the Christological formulas from Rom 1:3-4, and the hymnal "high Christology" of Phil 2:6-11; Col 1:15-20; Heb 1:1-4 and John 1:1-18.

Looking back, we see that the way which God came to and for humanity in and through Christ has indeed become visible: *The one God, who created the world and chose Israel to be his own people, sent his Son Jesus into the world, so that he could provide atonement for Israel through his way of suffering, prefigured by God in the Holy Scriptures, and accomplish, through his resurrection, justification in the last judgment for all who confess him to be Lord and Messiah.*

NOTES

1. For the opposing view cf. for example H. KOESTER, *Ancient Christian Gospels*, 1992[3]. following him is J. D. CROSSAN, *The Historical Jesus*, 1991.

2. Cf. R BULTMANN, *The History of the Synoptic Tradition* (1921), ET 1963[3].

3. Cf. M. DIBELIUS, *From Tradition to Gospel* (1919), ET 1965.

4. For classic examples of this view, see G. BORNKAMM, *Jesus of Nazareth* (1956), ET 1960, N. PERRIN, *Rediscovering the Teaching of Jesus*, 1967, and R. W. FUNK, R. W. HOOVER and the JESUS SEMINAR, *The Five Gospels*, 1993.

5. Cf. J. JEREMIAS, *Neutestamentliche Theologie, Erster Teil: Die Verkündigung Jesu*, 1973[2] (ET 1971), pp. 13-46.

6. Cf. M. BLACK, *An Aramaic Approach to the Gospels and Acts*, 1967[3].

7. Cf. E. E. ELLIS, "New Directions in Form Criticism" in his *Prophecy and Hermeneutics*, 1978 (reprint 1993) pp. 237-253, as well as "Gospel Criticism: A Perspective on the State of the Art," in *The Gospel and the Gospels*, P. STUHLMACHER (ed.), 1991, pp. 26-52.

8. Cf. B. GERHARDSSON, *Memory and Manuscript*, 1961, as well as his *The Origins of the Gospel Traditions*, 1977 ET 1979 and *The Gospel Tradition*, 1986.

9. Cf. M. HENGEL, "Jesus als messianischer Lehrer der Weisheit und die Anfänge der Christologie" in *Sagesse et religion* (Colloque de Strasbourg, Octobre 1976), 1979, pp. 148-188.

10. Cf. B. F. MEYER, *The Aims of Jesus*, 1979, and his *Christus Faber*, 1992.

11. Cf. H. RIESENFELD, "The Gospel Tradition and its beginnings," *TU* 73 (1959) pp. 43-65.

12. Cf. R. RIESNER, *Jesus als Lehrer*, 1988[3].

13. Cf. H. SCHÜRMANN, Jesus—Gestalt und Geheimnis, K. SCHOLTISSEK (ed.), 1994, pp. 380-389, 420-432.

14. In his book, *Heil als Geschichte*, 1967[2] (ET 1967), p.172, O. CULLMANN expects a post Easter construction only when the following conditions are met: "1. when this logion really contradicts another Jesus logion which is also present in the old tradition to such a degree that they are mutually exclusive; 2. when it presupposes a situation which is indeed unthinkable for the time of Jesus and his environment; 3. when a synoptic comparison suggests or insists that a logion was composed at a later date."

15. Cf. O. BETZ-R. RIESNER, *Jesus, Qumran and the Vatican. Clarifications* (1993) ET 1994, p. 91.

16. The same claim is made here in the synoptic tradition as is also documented John 5:21, 26.

17. Translation from the Revised Standard Version.

18. For the following cf. my article, "Der messianische Gottesknecht," *JBTh* 8 (1993) pp.131-154.

19. Cf. above all M. HENGEL, "Jesus der Messias Israels," in *Messiah and Christos. Studies in the Jewish Origins of Christianity*. FS for David Flusser in honor of his 75th birthday, L GRÜNWALD,

SHAKED, G. G. STROUMSA (eds.), 1992, pp. 155-176; (esp. pp. 165ff.).

20. Cf. J. BLINZLER, *Der Prozess Jesu*, 1969[4].

21. Cf. O. BETZ, "Probleme des Prozesses Jesu," *ANRW* II 25/1, 1982, pp. 565-647.

22. Cf. N A. DAHL, "The Crucified Messiah," in his *The Crucified Messiah*, 1974, pp. 10-36 (esp. 23ff.).

23. The most important of them was the *tamid*-sacrifice, which was offered mornings and evenings (cf. Exod 29:38-42; Num 28:3-8). This sacrifice was financed by the temple tax (a tax which only Jews were required to pay) and was intended to provide daily atonement for the sins of Israel (cf. Jub 6:14; 50:11).

24. J. ÅDNA in his dissertation *Jesu Kritik am Tempel*, Tübingen/Stavanger 1994 (unpublished) pp. 124ff., p. 573, points out how Mark 10.45 par. is to be seen in connection with the *tamid*-sacrifice and the cleansing of the temple.

25. P. 75.

26. For more detail on this cf. my *Biblische Theologie* vol. 1, 1992, p. 175ff.

3

THE TESTIMONY OF PAUL AND OF THE JOHANNINE SCHOOL

The letters of Paul and the Gospel of John belong, without a doubt, to the main books of the New Testament. A Biblical Theology of the New Testament must therefore place particular emphasis upon reproducing the testimony of these letters and the Fourth Gospel.

A. Paul and his School

Paul makes clear in his letters that he had received the "light of the knowledge of the glory of God in the face of Christ" at the point of his being called to become an apostle (cf. Gal 1:1, 11-17; 1 Cor 9:1; 15:8-10; 2 Cor 4:5-6; 5:16; Rom 1:1-5; Phil 3:7-11). The disciples of Paul, whose voices are heard (in Colossians), in Ephesians and in the Pastoral Epistles, confirm this (cf. Col 1:1, 25-28; Eph 3:1-7; 1 Tim 1:12-17; Tit 1:3).

1. *The calling of Paul*

According to Acts 22:3, Paul's Jewish theological education took place in Jerusalem, at the house of learning of the Rabbi Gamaliel.[1] If we let this information stand as valid, then Paul had experienced the events of Jesus' passion and the formation of the early Church in Jerusalem from a distance. From this perspective, he undertook to secure the judgment of those Jews who had fallen away and joined those already having faith in Christ. Faithfulness to the one God and the Torah, which he pursued with more militant zeal than many of his own age (cf. Gal 1:14), appeared to him to be incompatible with the confession of these apostates, ʼΙησοῦς Χριστός (= Jesus [and only he] is the Messiah!) and the acclamation, Κύριος ʼΙησοῦς (= Jesus [and only he] is the Lord!, cf. Ps 110:1), because Jesus, who was here being proclaimed "Messiah" and "Lord," had been condemned shortly before by the Jewish leaders in Jerusalem (cf. 1 Cor 2:8; Acts 3:17; 13:27) as a pseudo-messianic blasphemer and had died on a Roman cross under the curse of God, as such a man deserved (cf. Deut 21:23).

When Paul was surprised by the appearance of the risen Christ on the road to Damascus and thereby called to be an apostle, this experience helped him to a threefold realization.

1.1 Paul's experience of the risen Christ showed him that the crucified Jesus had truly been raised and glorified by God. Thus, the Christians whom Paul had persecuted up to this point were right before God with their confession: ʼΙησοῦς Χριστός, while he, despite his zeal for the Torah, was wrong and so was forced to accept the Christian confession as true and to correct his own understanding of Jesus (cf. 2 Cor 5:16).

1.2 The acceptance of this confession implied the second realization that God's will to save was from now on to be perceived first and foremost with a view to the risen Christ, and only secondarily to the Torah. The light of God's glory in the face of the risen Christ had shone more brightly than the glory of the Torah, which Paul had served up to that point (cf. 2 Cor 4:6 with 2 Cor 3:9).

1.3 When Paul realized at Damascus that the risen Christ, whom he had persecuted, had not destroyed him, but, contrary to all expectation, had absolved him and called him to be his apostle (cf. 2 Cor 2:14[2]), he experienced himself the merciful "acceptance" of the sinner through Christ (cf. Rom 15:7). He thus experienced the justification of the sinner (cf. Rom 4:5; 5:6) at a time when he was not yet able to teach it as doctrine. It becomes clear, when looking at this threefold recognition as a whole, *that the crucial content of the apostle's gospel of Jesus Christ and the justification of sinners through faith in this Christ was alone the result of the revelation at Damascus.* Paul did not become the proclaimer of the gospel of the justification of sinners gradually, as is suggested by some today, but was so because of his call and thus from that very day on, that God, "who. . .called me by his grace, was pleased to reveal his Son in me so that I might preach him among the Gentiles" (Gal 1:15-16).

2. *The Pauline gospel*

Paul, having been baptized and accepted into the Christian congregation at Damascus, now became acquainted from the inside with the teachings of the Christians, which to this point he had tried to destroy (cf. Gal 1:13). This gave him the possibility to formulate the threefold knowledge gained from his revelation experience (see above) in a language which harmonized with and was based upon these teachings. At the same time, he began to relate the Holy Scriptures to Christ and to the activity of the one God who had sent Jesus and raised him from the dead (cf. Rom 15:4). The teaching of Paul, therefore, proceeds from the revelation of the risen Christ at Damascus, but, with regard to its formulation, Paul latches on to the Christian traditions which preceded him, and then carries them further through his own Christological exegesis of the Holy Scriptures. Accordingly, he formulated the gospel as the *message of salvation concerning the righteousness of God in Christ.*

2.1 When Paul speaks of Jesus Christ, he seldom

coins independent and new formulations (cf., for example, Gal 3:13; 1 Cor 1:23-24; 2:2; Rom 10:4; 15:8-9). Much more often he latches onto Christological traditions and formulas which he had learned from the Christians in Damascus, Jerusalem and the missionary church at Antioch, where he had been active for one year prior to his longer missionary journeys (cf. Acts 11:26). Examples can already be found in 1 Thess (cf. 4:14; 5:9). Others are in the letter to the Galatians (cf. Gal 1:4; 4:4), in the two letters to the Corinthians (cf. 1 Cor 1:30; 6:11; 11:23-25; 15:3-5; 2 Cor 5:21), in Romans (cf. Rom 1:3-4; 3:24-26; 4:25; 6:3-4; 8:3, 15, 34; 15:3), as well as in Philippians and Colossians (cf. Phil 2:6-11 and Col 1:15-20). This procedure can also be seen in the school of the apostle (cf. Eph 1:20-23; 2:4-6, 11-12; 1 Tim 2:5-6; 3:16; 6:13; 2 Tim 1:9-10; 2:8; Tit 3:4-7). This finding has sometimes been understood as an indication that Paul and his school had developed no independent interest in Christology, but were "just citing tradition." The main interest of the apostle was, according to this theory, not Christology, but the theology of the cross and anthropology. Already GEORG EICHHOLZ[3] came against this interpretation, which was championed by the school of RUDOLF BULTMANN and even today has not been fully overcome.[4] This interpretation is false and is a great hindrance to an understanding of Paul from the perspective of Biblical Theology. Two points must be made in rejecting it.

2.1.1 As a Jew and Jewish-Christian, Paul did not have a negative concept of tradition, but a positive one. The apostle and his disciples, therefore, argue not against the tradition, but *with it,* because they are interested in the continuity of the apostolic teachings which runs "from the Lord" (ἀπὸ τοῦ κυρίου) to the Jerusalem apostles, and then on to the school of Paul (cf. 1 Cor 11:23; 15:1-3, 11; Rom 6:17). Paul even criticizes his opponents for teaching "another Jesus" (cf. 2 Cor 11:4) and "another gospel" (cf. Gal 1:6-9), while claiming, on the other hand, that he proclaims the one Christ who died on the cross "for us" and was raised by God. This is identical with the one εὐαγγέλιον τοῦ Χριστοῦ, without which all faith is useless (cf. 1 Cor 15:14). It is thus consistent with Paul's thinking when 1 Tim 6:20 and 2 Tim 1:12-14 emphasize that everything depends on the unadulterated transmission of the gospel (handed down by Paul), because this gospel is the "good deposit" (παραθήκη) which has been given through revelation and must therefore be preserved for the coming generations.

2.1.2 As Gal 4:4; 1 Cor 15:20-28; Rom 1:1-6; 9:5; 11:25-31; 15:8-9 demonstrate and as is emphasized *expressis verbis* in Colossians and Ephesians (cf. Col 1:25; Eph 1:10; 3:2, 9), the gospel of God concerning Jesus Christ leads to the knowledge of God's salvation plan, the οἰκονομία τοῦ θεοῦ: The one God who created the world and chose Israel to be his own people, proclaimed through his prophets the coming of the messianic Son; as the time had been fulfilled, he sent his (pre-existent) Son into the world; in accordance with the promise (of 2 Sam 7:12-14[5]), this Son of God descends as a man from the Davidic family, and, after completing his way of suffering, he was raised from the dead by his Heavenly Father and appointed "Son of God in power" (Rom 1:4). The eschatological salvation of both Jews and Gentiles has its guarantee in him, for he must continue his heavenly reign till all the enemies of God, including death, are overcome and forced to praise God (cf. Phil 2:10 with Isa 45:23[6]). When "the fullness of the Gentiles" (cf. Gen 10:1-32; 1 Chron 1:1-54[7]) have entered into the holy congregation (Rom 11:25), he will appear from Zion, in accordance with the promise (cf. Isa 45:17, 25), to save "all Israel" (Rom 11:26) from unbelief and to initiate for Jews and Gentiles the glorious freedom of the children of God in the midst of a creation which has been freed from its vanity. It is not difficult to recognize that the structures of this "economy of salvation" are taken, for the most part, from the Holy Scriptures.

3. *The Pauline doctrine of justification*

Paul's doctrine of justification is considered to be peculiar to Paul, and rightly so. This view should not, however, disguise the fact that the roots of this doctrine are already to be found in pre-Pauline Christianity, and from there reach on back to the preaching of Jesus (cf. Luke 18:9-14 and Mark 8:37 par. [cf. with Ps 49:8-9] and 10:45 par.), ancient Judaism and the Holy Scriptures. If one would like to express in one sentence what Paul means when he speaks of justification, one must speak of *the accomplishment of the righteousness of God in and through Christ.*

3.1 In the Old Testament, the righteousness of God is a concept of salvation. It designates the conduct of God, the creator, that produces salvation and benevolent order (cf. for example Ps 98:2, 9; Isa 45:8). Also, when the expression is used in the context of temporal or eternal judgment, it does not lose its positive sense, for God judges in such a way that the poor and those with no rights are vindicated (cf. Ps 35:23-24, 27). Thus the Jewish penitential Psalms appeal to God's righteousness as the very essence of his grace and mercy (cf. Neh 9:8, 17, 33; Dan 9:7, 16; 4 Esd 8:34-36). In 1 QS 11:11-15, the petitioner, deeply aware of his lowliness and sin, praises the righteousness of God (צדקת אל) as the creative mercy and goodness of God which cleanses from sin.[8] The Jewish-Christian paradosis[9] which Paul uses in Rom 3:25-36 (and 2 Cor 5:21) had taken over this use of the term δικαιοσύνη θεοῦ, and Paul, too, follows it in Rom 1:17; 3:21-26; 10:3 (cf. also Phil 3:9).

3.2 For the later parts of the Old Testament, the early Jewish apocalyptic, and the New Testament, the whole world is seen in the context of the impending last judgment, at which time the abysmal antithesis between God's holiness and the unholiness of the whole sinful creation will be made manifest and then be overcome. The biblical teachings regarding justification can not be understood apart from this background. Within this context, justification (δι–καίωσις) means to be absolved from all sins before the judgment seat of God and then to enter into His kingdom. Paul also thinks in this way. According to his gospel, God himself in his mercy laid the foundation for the justification of all sinners in the face of the impending last judgment, because before the judgment throne of God (or Christ) (cf. 2 Cor 5:10; Rom 14:10) they have nothing to offer which could redeem them, not even the cultic sin offerings, which had lost their meaning through Jesus' death on the cross, nor their own deeds of obedience with respect to the Law.[10] Through the sending and the delivering over of his Son to die, He brought about atonement once and for all, and through the raising up of Jesus, He made this atonement effective for the last days. Whoever believes in Jesus Christ, confesses the crucified Christ raised by God as Savior and Lord, and follows his instruction, will gain a part in the righteousness effected through Jesus' way of sacrifice (2 Cor 5:21). He or she can, furthermore, be certain of the intercession of the Exalted One before God's throne up to and including the time of the last judgment (cf. Rom 8:34). In Rom 8:31-34, Paul gives unsurpassed expression to the assurance of salvation characteristic of the belief in God's righteousness:

> [31]...If God is for us, who is against us? [32]He who did not spare his own Son but gave him up for us all, will he not also give us all things with him? [33]Who shall bring any charge against God's elect? It is God who justifies; [34]Who is to condemn? Is it Christ Jesus, who died, yes, who was raised from the dead, who is at the right hand of God, who indeed intercedes for us?[11]

According to Romans, the righteousness effected by God in and through Jesus for all believers is the central content of the gospel (cf. Rom 1:16-17; 3:21-26), and, according to Phil 3:9, the final salvation (or perdition) of every single person, including Paul's, is dependent upon this justification.

3.3 The biblical contours of this view are not difficult to recognize. The concepts of the righteousness of God and the expectation of the last judgment have their origin in the Old Testament to the same degree as does their Christological language. They are based on Isa 53:11 and include the recognition that the institution of atonement, initiated by God, was perfected and surpassed through Jesus' way of sacrifice (cf. Rom 3:25-26 with Lev 16:15; 17:11 and Rom 8:3 with Lev 4:3, 14, 21). Paul expands the range of his justification concept even further when he views the crucified and exalted Christ not only as the personification of this righteousness, sanctification and redemption initiated by God, but also, in application of Ps 8:7 and 110:1, as having been appointed to complete the messianic work of establishing the kingdom of God (cf. 1 Cor 15:20-28). According to Rom 8:18-30 and 11:25-32, the salvation of all of Israel also is a part of this work (as promised by God, for example, in Isa 45:17, 25), as is the liberation of the creation from the curse of vanity. *The realization of the righteousness of God in and through Christ has the same breadth as the mystery of God's economy of salvation just outlined, and thus Paul's proclamation of the establishment of this righteousness of God includes not only a part, but the whole of his theology.*

The students of Paul attempted to champion the eschatological perspectives which he handed down to them, as well as the understanding of the death of Jesus within the context of an atonement-theology and the concept of justification only through faith. This they did even though they were not confronted with the same opponents as their teacher nor did the questions concerning justification and law have the same acute relevance for them as for the apostle. Their attempts can be clearly seen in (a further interpretation of Col 1:20 and 3:24-29) Eph 1:3-14; 2:1-18,[12] as well as in such instructional texts as 1 Tim 1:5-6 and Tit 3:3-7. Thus, we can by no means speak of an abandonment of the Pauline inheritance by the pupils of Paul, and before undertaking—as is usually done—to criticize the fixation of this inheritance in doctrinal formulas by the school of Paul, one should consider the fact that the original Pauline gospel would not have been passed down to us in an unadulterated form had it not been for the work of the school of Paul.

B. The School of John

The testimony of the Johannine writings in the New Testament is of the same theological importance as the letters of Paul, but it presents the exegetes with even bigger problems than does the interpretation of Paul's letters. The question concerning the relationship between the Gospel of John, the three letters of John and the Revelation of John are historically (almost) unsolvable. The question, however, must be addressed because the historical dimension, and thus also an understanding of the circumstances surrounding the composition of the New Testament books, is an important part of a Biblical Theology of the New Testament. This is so because such a theology intends to trace, in a historically concrete way and not just in abstract dogmatic statements, the path which God took in coming to humanity in and through Christ, and to discover the actual original meaning of the New Testament books.

1. *The relationship of the Johannine writings to one another*

The picture of the Johannine writings usually sketched by scholarship today is so inexact that it does not make understanding the original meaning of the Johannine texts any easier, but makes it more difficult and cries out for revision.

1.1 Taking a look at the situation in Johannine scholarship,[13] one can describe this common view as follows: The Gospel of John represents the core of the Johannine tradition, while the letters of John are considered to be "letters produced by the school of the Evangelist,"[14] which were written long after the Gospel. The characteristic terminology and style common to the Gospel and the letters, but setting them apart from the Synoptics[15] or Pauline writings, are judged to be a Johannine soziolect, i.e., a "school language" used by the Johannine circle for theological communication. This soziolect renders the literary distinction between tradition and redaction in the Johannine writings very difficult. Since, however, the Gospel exhibits clear signs of a redaction,[16] many exegetes do not let this deter them from proposing sometimes wide-reaching critical theories about the redactional layers and editing of the Gospel of John (and the letters). Opinions vary with regard to the relationship between the Gospel of John and the Synoptic Gospels. One either assumes that the author was aware of at least the Gospels of Mark and Luke, or considers John to be almost completely independent of the synoptic tradition. With regard to chronology, the "school" of John is placed at the end of the first century, but the questions concerning where the school was centered or the author of the Gospel and letters is left undecided. The Revelation of John, which is much different than the Gospel and letters with regard to language and content, is usually considered far removed from them and attributed to an otherwise unknown prophet from Asia Minor called John. Recently, it is again held to be a pseudonymous writing (see p. 41ff.). Finally, scholars generally agree that the ancient Church of the second century was the first to attribute all Johannine writings to John the Zebedee.

1.2 If one desires to move beyond this picture with its many unanswered questions, one must (and can) proceed in a more historically precise manner.[17] Just by taking into account that the ancient Church's claim since Ireneus that John the Zebedee authored all of the Johannine writings is not simply arbitrary, and by noting that the second and third letters of John are authored by "the Elder" (ὁ πρεσβύτερος; cf. 2 John 1; 3 John 1), one begins to see the need to modify the picture of Johannine tradition sketched above. As has long been established,[18] it seems a natural conclusion to identify the presbyter from 2 John 1 and 3 John 1 with the "presbyter John" (ὁ πρεσβύτερος Ἰωάννης) mentioned by Papias of Hierapolis around 130 CE (in his work on the exegesis of the words of the Lord from which Eusebius, h.e. 3, 39, 4, quotes[19]). Papias clearly sets him apart from John the Zebedee, but still calls him "the disciple of the Lord" (τοῦ κυρίου μαθητής). Since Papias himself had met the presbyter, he must have been living in Asia Minor at the end of the first century. John the Zebedee, on the other hand, had already died, because he—as Papias and several other Church Fathers testify—was killed "by the Jews" and thus became a martyr like his brother James (cf. Acts 12:1-2).[20] Now if, because of the common language, one attributes not only the second and third, but all three Johannine letters as well as the Gospel to a common author,[21] and considers that, according to 21:20-23, the author of the Gospel lived to reach an old age, then *the author of the Johannine writings cannot refer to the martyred John the Zebedee, but only to John the Presbyter*: One would then assume that he was the head of the Johannine school, which was active in Asia Minor (Ephesus) till the end of the first century. If this is correct, one should make the historical assumption that the letters, which were composed during the lifetime of the "Elder," were written before the final redaction of the Gospel, since in John 21:23 the death of its author is presupposed.

1.3. If one wants to determine the place of the Revelation of John within the picture just constructed, then one must proceed from the assumption that Revelation is, according to Rev 1:4; 22:21, intended as a "letter" which John, who is openly named in 1:4; 22:8, has had sent to the seven churches in Asia Minor (and from there to the whole of the Church).[22] Since this John in Rev 22:9 is counted among the prophets and not among the twelve apostles mentioned in Rev 18:20; 21:14, but was well enough known in Asia Minor that he could expect his "letter" to be accepted, this John, as well, can hardly refer to any person other than John the Presbyter, from whom Papias had spoken. The reason for his exile on the island of Patmos (cf. Rev 1:9) could perhaps be sought in the controversies which led to the exclusion of the Johannine group from the synagogue (cf. John 9:22; 12:42; 16:2). The consciously Hebraized language of Revelation is, of course, thoroughly different than the "soziolect" of the letters and the Gospel, but in its choice of images and, to a certain degree, in vocabulary, it conforms strangely to it. At the same time, many (Christological) traditions in the Revelation of John are presented in a form which appears to be older than the corresponding statements in the Gospels and the letters. Thus, a complex relationship exists between traditions in the Johannine writings which can only be sorted out in a very hypothetical fashion.

In a way similar to GEORG STRECKER,[23] JÖRG FREY, in his informative and instructive "Erwägungen zum Verhältnis der Johannesapokalypse zu den übrigen Schriften im Corpus Johanneum," which has been published as an appendix to M. HENGEL's monograph, *Die johanneische Frage*,[24] comes to the conclusion that, although the Revelation is a product of the Johannine circle, it is a "pseudoepigraphon," first "attributed to the influential and well-known John from Asia Minor. . . in the redactional layer."[25] HENGEL holds this view as very plausible,[26] but, at the same time, considers whether the writing could not have been "produced by a member of the Johannine school using older apocalyptic fragments."[27] This is a view which can be more precisely developed from a traditio-historical perspective. Strikingly, the linguistic characteristics common to Revelation and the other Johannine writings are concentrated in the "epistolary frame" (i.e. in Rev 1:1-3:22 and 22:6-21), which surrounds the larger main core. In this main part the similarities are sparse. Thus, the Revelation of John could be a new edition of an older apocalyptic work which had been cherished in the Johannine school along with the Jesus tradition collected in the Gospel and was updated by adding the frame in 1:1-3:22 and 22:6-21.[28] One avoids with this view STRECKER and FREY's characterization of Revelation as a pseudoepigraphon, which runs totally contrary to Rev 1:1, 4; 22:8, 10, 21.

1.4 As a result of the preceding discussion, the following can serve as a basis for the exegesis of the Johannine writings. The "school" of John (in Asia Minor), which produced all of these writings, seems to be based upon a twofold foundation of tradition: First, it rests upon a gospel tradition, the origins of which reach back to John the Presbyter (who was a pupil of John the Zebedee).[29] However, in the course of discussions within the Johannine circle, the tradition was, in contrast to the synoptic tradition, newly formulated and arranged (into Christological texts of pedagogical character) by John the Presbyter and members of his school, who acted in the authority given them through the knowledge of the truth provided by the "Paraclete" (cf. John 14:16-17, 26; 16:13). These catechetical texts were collected in the Gospel of John, which was edited by the school of the presbyter after his death at the end of the first century. In editing it, they viewed the elder John and John the Zebedee together as the ideal type of the "disciple whom Jesus loved" (cf. John 1:35-40; 13:23; 19:26; 20:2; 21:7, 20), thus immortalizing them.[30] In the last decade of the first century, the Revelation of John, which had been published by order of John the Presbyter, appears on the scene as the other part of the Johannine school tradition (a tradition which can also be traced back in part to John the Zebedee?). It speaks of the work of the exalted Christ, the travail of the end times, and the impending universal judgment. The three Johannine letters were also written during the lifetime of the presbyter, which makes them older than the Gospel or Revelation.[31] They mirror the disputes which had erupted within the Johannine school when part of the Johannine pupils began to separate themselves from the others and to subscribe to docetic views. The reaction to this schism exerted a great influence upon the development of the Johannine Christology and tradition of faith. However, the separation from synagogal Judaism, which had forced the (originally completely Jewish-christian) Johannine circle out of its community over the years, also contributed to this development (John 9:22; 12:42; 16:2; Rev 2:9; 3:9).[32]

It is characteristic of the thought of the Johannine school that it carefully preserves the tradition of the Revelation on the one hand, but, on the other, takes the opportunity afforded by the disputes in which it was involved to reflect more fundamentally than the Synoptic Gospels on the relationship of God the Father, the Son and the Holy Spirit, of the present and the future, of salvation and judgment and of the Church and the world. The insights gained thereby become first visible in the Johannine letters, but then also influenced the Johannine gospel tradition.

2. *The Johannine Christology*

The decisive contribution of the school of John for Biblical Theology is the development of a Logos-Christology. The Johannine writings speak of this in a threefold manner.

2.1 From the perspective of tradition history, the oldest layer is probably to be found in the description of Christ from Rev 19:11-16 (21), which bears the stamp of the Old Testament and apocalyptic in every way. Here Christ appears for the universal judgment at the head of the armies of heaven, sits upon a white war horse, is dressed in the robe of God, stained with blood (cf. Isa 63:2-3), and fights and defeats with the sword of his mouth the wicked

Gentile nations (cf. Jes 11:4; Ps 2:9). Upon the belt on his loins (cf. Isa 11:5) is written "King of Kings and Lord of Lords." However, his main name is, "the Word of God" (ὁ λόγος τοῦ θεοῦ, Rev 19:13). This designation may well come from WisSol 18:14-16[33]: Christ, who overcomes the enemies of God at the end of time, is the personification of the word of God, because through him God makes himself known to the world by having his Son judge all who would rebel against his holy will.

2.2 In 1 John 1:1-4 the author of the letter proclaims to his readers that Christ is "word of life" (ὁ λόγος τῆς ζωῆς). From the very beginning he was with the Father, was revealed on the earth, and the presbyter had personally heard, seen and (before and after Easter) touched him with his own hands (cf. John 13:23; 20:20). He is called "word of life" because he, in his divine person, makes eternal life available to those who are joined with him through the community of faith (cf. 1 John 5:10-11). In 1 John 1:1-4, Christ is no longer the Christ of the parousia as in Rev 19, but is the pre-existent, incarnated, exalted and proclaimed Son of God. He makes up the substantial content of the Johannine witness, because he is the gospel of God personified.[34]

> The statements in 1 John 1:1-4 are not identical with John 1:1-18, but the school tradition of the Johannine circle assembled in the Fourth Gospel is already emerging. This school tradition deals only secondarily with Jesus' earthly existence. Its main intention is to describe the character and work of the exalted Christ present in the Church and to show that eternal life only comes through encountering him and remaining in his word. (cf. John 15:1- 8; 20:30-31)

2.3 In the prologue of John (John 1:1-18) we find that layer of the Logos-Christology which, more that any other, was responsible for its lasting influence. The extant text of the prologue very probably grew out of the adaptation of an artistically composed hymn in which Christ is praised as the personified Word of God and is called simply ὁ λόγος "the Word."[35] The provenance of this title is also the wisdom literature and it teaches to confess Christ as the personification of God's creative word (cf. WisSol 9:1-4).[36] In Christ, the Logos, who has God's divine nature, reveals himself as God of the world, as creator and savior, so that through him the world may encounter God and receive eternal life. The main Christological interest of the Logos-hymn lies in the divine nature of the Logos, his incarnation and the revelation of God's mercy which occurs through him.

2.3.1 The profound theological reflection of the Johannine school in John 1:1-18 is evident in the fact that the hymn was developed into a three-part prologue to the Gospel, in which, besides the elements just mentioned, the reaction of the world to the Logos is dealt with. The appearance of the Logos on the earth leads either to rejection or faith. In 1:1-5 the existence and work of the Logos before, during, and after the creation of the world are described. Then, in John 1:6-8 (the Synoptics being used as a model), John the Baptist is introduced as the earthly forerunner of the Christ-Logos. Following this, the coming of the Logos into the world is reported *twice*. The theme of 1:9-13 is the appearance and rejection of the Logos in the world (with which most probably Israel is indicated); only a small minority—the "disciple whom Jesus loved" and the presbyter being among this group—accepted him and were bestowed with the status of children of God (cf. 1:12-13). Then, in 1:14-18, the prologue once again speaks of the appearance of the Christ-Logos on earth, but now under the aspect of his *recognition* by these (and all) believers. They confess in 1:14-18 that the Logos became flesh, lived among "us," made known to "us" the glory of God, and is even greater than Moses, because and in that he is the only begotten son and revealer of God.

2.3.2 By way of the believers' confession in the first person plural that the Logos is the μονογενὴς θεός (1:18), the boundary between the pre-Easter work of Jesus and the post-Easter activity of the Exalted One is broken through. Thus, Jesus Christ appears as the divine word of the creator, in whom God, for all time, reveals himself to the world.

2.3.3 The Fourth Gospel describes this *Christus praesens* in such a way that, while knowledge of the synoptic tradition among the readers (above all, as it appears in Mark and Luke) is assumed,[37] the synoptic presentation is constantly given new and different accents. These are not only to be found in the new arrangement of the Gospel, the revelation and farewell discourses, and the reports of the miraculous signs of Jesus, but also in the daring change in date of Jesus' death on a cross to the day before the Passover (Nisan 14) and the new passion narrative. In contrast to the Synoptics, the way of sacrifice traversed by Jesus no longer only fulfills the Scriptures (cf. John 19:24, 28-29), but also Jesus' own prophecy concerning his death (cf. John 18:8-9, 31-32). Jesus dies no longer after six hours on the cross, but after only three (cf. 19:14). His last words on the cross were not, as according to Mark and Matthew (following Ps 22:2): "My God, My God, why have you forsaken me?" (Mark 15:34; Matt 27:46), or (following Ps 31:6): "Father, into your hands I commit my spirit" (Luke 23:46), but "It is finished" (John 19:30). This τετέλεσται reminds the reader of the Gospel of Isa 55:11 and Gen 2:1-2: The creation word has completed its way and the work of the new creation of the world has been accomplished through the establishment of faith (cf. 3:16).[38] Consistent with this is also the fact that the Fourth Gospel deviates from the synoptic narrative in 19:38-41 by reporting that Jesus was given a complete and honorable burial at the hands of Joseph of Arimathea and Nicodemus already on Good Friday. The Christ-Logos may thus rest in his tomb from his work on the Sabbath following his burial, as God rested on the seventh day after the completion of six days of work (cf.

Gen 2:2). He rises from his rest in the tomb "on the first day of the week" (20:1), orders Mary of Magdala not to keep him from returning to the Father (20:17), and finally, on the evening of this day, appears (from his place with the Father) to his frightened disciples in order to send them out to carry on his mission and to give them the Holy Spirit, which gives understanding with respect to his teachings (cf.14:26) and bestows upon them the "office of the keys," i.e. the authority to forgive sins or to retain them (cf. 20:19-23).

C. Summary

Looking back upon the preaching of the schools of Paul and of John, we note that both played a decisive role in the development of the New Testament witness to Christ. As different as the language of the two schools may be, the confession which they both hold high is clear: God reveals himself in the world only through his only Son, who is the Christ; only through his sacrifice and resurrection from the dead is salvation in the last days made available to Jews and Gentiles; the only way to this salvation is to believe in him, and this faith includes the confession of Jesus as Lord as well as obedience to his instruction (cf. 1 John 4:7-14; John 13:34-35; Gal 5:6; 1 Cor 13).

NOTES

1. For Paul's early life cf. M. HENGEL, *The Pre-Christian Paul,* 1991, and R. RIESNER, *Die Frühzeit des Apostels Paulus,* 1994, pp. 31-65.

2. For background information to 2 Cor 2:14 cf. S. HAFEMANN, *Suffering and the Spirit*, 1986, 12-39 (in the revised American edition, 1990, pp. 16-34).

3. Cf. G. EICHHOLZ, *Die Theologie des Paulus im Umriss,* 1972, pp. 7-13.

4. It lives on in views of E. P. SANDERS regarding Pauline Christology; cf. his *Paul* 1991, pp. 77-83.

5. For the connection between Rom 1:3-4 and Nathan's prophecy cf., above all, O. BETZ, *Was wissen wir von Jesus*? (rev. ed.) 1991 (ET 1967), pp. 110ff.

6. That Phil 2:10 is to be interpreted eschatologically, has been shown by O. HOFIUS, *Der Christushymnus Philipper* 2:6-11, 1991[2], pp. 18-55.

7. For Paul's view of the Gentile peoples cf. the monograph by J. M. SCOTT, *Paul and the Nations* to be published 1995 in the WUNT Series edited by M. HENGEL and O. HOFIUS.

8. According to the translation by G. VERMES, *The Dead Sea Scrolls in English*, 1987[3], pp. 78f. this passage reads as follows:

> As for me,
> if I stumble, the mercies of God
> shall be my eternal salvation.
> If I stagger because of the sin of flesh,
> my justification shall be
> by the righteousness of God which endures for ever.
> When my distress is unleashed
> He will deliver my soul from the Pit
> and will direct my steps to the way.
> He will draw me near by His grace,
> and by His mercy will he bring my justification.
> He will judge me in the righteousness of His truth
> and in the greatness of His goodness
> He will pardon all my sins.
> Through His righteousness he will cleanse me
> of the uncleanness of man
> and of the sins of the children of men,
> that I may confess to God His righteousness,
> and His majesty to the Most High.

9. Cf. for the characterization of 2 Cor 5:21 and Rom 3:25-26 as tradition, my *Biblische Theologie*, vol. 1, pp. 193ff., 296ff.

10. The hope that works of the law would establish righteousness before God is clearly expressed in the early Jewish text, 4Q MMT 21:3, 7-8; 4 Esra 9:7. So when Paul states that the works of the law cannot lead to righteousness (Gal 2:16; Rom 3:20 cf. with Ps 143:2), he is not constructing a distorted picture of early Jewish expectation regarding justification, as is often held today. This can also be seen in the polemic of James 2:24 against the Pauline position.

11. Translation from the Revised Standard Version.

12. It seems that in both texts the tradition of Col 1:15-20; 3:24-29 has been taken over and interpreted.

13. This summary is based on the following works: W. G KÜMMEL, *Introduction to the New Testament* (1963) ET 1975; P. VIELHAUER, *Geschichte der urchristlichen Literatur* 1975; E. LOHSE, *Entstehung des Neuen Testaments*, 1975; G. STRECKER, *Litera-*

turgeschichte des Neuen Testaments, 1992; H CONZELMANN-A. LINDEMANN, *Interpreting the New Testament* (1975) ET 1988; as well as the commentaries on the Gospel of John, the Letters of John and Revelation from C. K. BARRETT, J. BECKER, R. BROWN, E. HAENCHEN, R. SCHNACKENBURG, H-J. KLAUCK, J. ROLOFF, G. STRECKER, and others.

14. H. CONZELMANN, *Grundriss der Theologie des Neuen Testaments*, 1987[4] (ET 1969), (ed.) A. LINDEMANN, p. 360.

15. The one exception being Luke 10:21-22/Matt 11:25-27.

16. Cf., for example, the topographically strange order of John 5 and 6, which already disturbed Tatian; the insertion of John 15-17 between 14:31 and 18:1; the addition of cap. 21 to 20:30-31, which had concluded the Gospel, and the glosses in 3:24; 4:2; 18:9, 32.

17. The following is based on M. HENGEL's thoughts on the question, presented first in his Stone Lectures: *The Johannine Question*, 1989, and then in considerably enlarged and partially revised form in his monograph, *Die johanneische Frage*, 1993.

18. Cf., for example, W. KÜMMEL, *Einleitung*[19], p. 209.

19. M. Hengel translates the Papias-fragment cited by Eusebius as follows: "And if anyone chanced to come who had actually been a follower of the elders, I would inquire as to the discourses of the elders, what Andrew or what Peter said, or what Philip, or what Thomas or James, or what John or Matthew or any other of the Lord's disciples; and the things which Aristion and John the elder, the disciples of the Lord say" (*The Johannine Question* [see n. 17] p. 17.).

20. Cf. HENGEL, *Die johanneische Frage* [see N. 17] pp. 88ff. Rev 10:3-13 is possibly intended to be a reference to the martyrdoms of the two Zebedees.

21. Cf. E. RUCKSTUHL-P. DSCHULNIGG, *Stilkritik und Verfasserfrage im Johannesevangelium*, 1991.

22. For a treatment of Revelation of John as "letter," cf. M. KARRER, *Die Johannesoffenbarung als Brief*, 1986 and J. ROLOFF, *Die Offenbarung des Johannes*, 1984.

23. *Literaturgeschichte* (cf. n. 13), pp. 274f.

24. Ibid, 326-429.

25. Ibid, 425.

26. Ibid, 334.

27. Ibid, 334.

28. G. EISENKOLB in her article "Endlich schliesst die Offenbarung dann das ganze Bibelbuch" in the Schülerfestschrift for F. Mildenberger on his 65th birthday, *Zeitworte*, (eds.) H. ASSEL, K. EBERLEIN, F. HECKMANN, H. HÖVELMANN, 1994, pp. 224-234, following HENGEL (*Die joh. Frage* [cf. n. 17], 315ff.), assumes a teacher-pupil relationship between John the Presbyter and John the Zebedee. She constructs the following perspective (which must be further developed) for the authorship of Revelation: "The Presbyter re-

ceived a copy of the original apocalypse from his teacher John the Zebedee before his martyrdom (or from his literary remains). Through the preaching of this disciple he would have been familiar with the language and imagery of the apocalypse. Despite the accentual changes which he brought about in the Johannine theology, he remembered the apocalyptic text while in exile, carefully revised it and brought it to the attention of the churches by way of the open letter" (ibid.230).

29. Cf. HENGEL, *Die joh. Frage* [cf. n. 17], pp. 317f.

30. Cf. HENGEL, *Die joh. Frage* [cf. n. 17], pp. 313-320.

31. For this view, which is also taken by J. G. STRECKER, cf. HENGEL, *Die joh. Frage* [cf. n. 17], pp. 155ff.

32. The reason for this break could lie in the clear confession of the Johannine circle to the divinity of Jesus Christ (cf. John 1:1,18; 20:28; 1 John 1:2).

33. The translation of WisSol 18:14-16 in the New American Bible, 1986, reads as follows:

> [14]For when peaceful stillness compassed everything
> and the night in its swift course was half spent,
> [15]Your all-powerful word from heaven's royal throne
> bounded, a fierce warrior, into the doomed land,
> [16]bearing the sharp sword of your inexorable decree.
> And as he alighted, he filled every place with death;
> he still reached to heaven, while he stood upon the earth.

34. One should note the interesting terminological parallelism between 1 John 1:1 and Phil 2:16. Also, in Acts 10:36-43 Christ is the gospel of God personified.

35. For a reconstruction of this hymn, cf. O. Hofius, "Struktur und Gedankengang des Logos-Hymnus in John 1:1-18" *ZNW* 78 (1978) pp.1-25.

36. The sapiential background of the Johannine prologue have been pointed out by H. GESE in his article, "The Prologue to John's Gospel" in his *Essays on Biblical Theology* (1977), ET 1981, pp. 167-222 (esp. 190ff.).

37. For the similarities between Mark, Luke and the Fourth Gospel cf. C. K. BARRETT, *The Gospel according to St. John*, 1978[2], pp. 42-54.

38. Cf. M. HENGEL, "Die Schriftauslegung des 4. Evangeliums auf dem Hintergrund der urchristlichen Exegese," *JBTH*4 (1989) pp. 249-288 (esp. 284ff.).

4

THE CHRISTIAN CANON, ITS CENTER, AND ITS INTERPRETATION

A Biblical Theology of the New Testament which attempts to trace the path which God took to humanity in and through Christ cannot be satisfied with a description of the witness of the Gospels, the school of Paul, and the school of John (or of the other books of the New Testament), but must also show how it came to the formation of the two-part Christian canon of the Old and New Testaments, whether this canon has a theological center, and how it wants to be interpreted. Since Biblical Theology takes the canon as her starting point and examines its individual writings, she must return to this point at the conclusion of her work if she intends to complete her task.

1. *The formation of the Christian canon*

Looking at things from a New Testament perspective, there are two things which led to the formation of the biblical canon: All authors of the New Testament presuppose that the one God and Father of Jesus Christ, who speaks to the Church of Jesus Christ through the Holy Scriptures (of the Old Testament), has only in the person of Jesus Christ fully and finally revealed himself to Jews and Gentiles. This conviction finds its classic expression in Heb 1:1-2:

> In many and various ways God spoke of old to our fathers by the prophets, but in these last

> days he has spoken to us by a Son, whom he appointed to be heir of all things, through whom also he created the world.[1]

Therefore, if the whole of God's revelation is to become clearly known, then—first—the prophets (and with them, all of the Holy Scriptures) must be brought into relation with God's act of salvation through his Son and—second—the Holy Scriptures are to be enlarged to include the direct witnesses of this saving act. Or to put it in a different way: The saving word of God is only fully heard when the γραφαὶ ἅγιαι are understood in the light of the appearance of Jesus Christ and read together with the witness of the apostles.

1.1 The application of the Holy Scriptures to the saving act of God in and through Jesus Christ is characteristic of all New Testament writings.

1.1.1 As we have already seen, the core of the Holy Scriptures at the time of the formation of New Testament tradition consisted of—as Luke 24:44 puts it—"the Law of Moses and the Prophets and the Psalms." It is therefore no surprise that the New Testament quotations from and allusions to the Old Testament are taken for the most part from these books.

> According to the index of citations and allusions in the 27th edition of Nestle (-Aland), the Prophets are *directly cited* around 180 times (the largest number from Isaiah) the Torah around 150 times (the most from Deuteronomy), and the Psalms about 55 times. There are occasional quotes from Sirach (cf. Mark 10:19; James 1:19), Ascension of Isaiah (cf. 1 Cor 2:9[2]), and 1 (Ethiopic Apocalypse of) Enoch (cf. Jude 14-15). Chronicles, Ezra, Esther, Song of Songs, Lamentations, and Ecclesiastes are hardly mentioned at all.—When Old Testament allusions appear, they, too, come mainly from the Prophets, Torah and Psalms, and (only) occasionally from Sirach, WisSol or 1 Hen—

> Constituting the core of the Holy Scriptures used by the New Testament are, thus, Torah, Prophets and Psalms, while Sir, WisSol and 1 Hen (among others) appear only on the periphery.[3]

The problem for the early Christian authors does not (yet) lie in defining the boundaries of the Old Testament, but *in applying it to God's act of salvation in and through Jesus Christ.*

1.1.2 In applying the Holy Scriptures, they are read as witnesses according to the following principle: "...everything that was written in the past was written to teach us, so that through...the encouragement of the Scriptures we might have hope" (Rom 15:4). The methods of early Christian exegesis of the Old Testament closely parallel Jewish prototypes, as found, for example, in the commentaries on the Prophets at Qumran or in the Rabbinic Halakah and in the Midrashim. Especially pronounced is the typological reading of the Holy Scriptures (cf. 1 Cor 10:11).[4] Early Christianity shares the view with ancient Judaism that the γραφαὶ ἅγιαι are inspired by the Spirit of God (cf. Mark 12:36 par.; John 5:39; 12:38-41; Acts 4:25; 1 Cor 10:11; 2 Cor 3:16-17; 2 Tim 3:16; Heb 3:7-11; 10:15-17; 1 Pet 1:11; 2 Pet 1:20-21).[5] The main difference to the Jewish understanding of Scripture is that for the New Testament the Spirit which fills the Scriptures is not just the Spirit of God, who reveals himself to Israel and the whole world in the instruction which proceeds from Sinai, but the Spirit of the Father of Jesus Christ and the exalted Christ himself. The Christian Church therefore reads the inspired Holy Scriptures with their eyes having been opened by the risen Christ and the Spirit which he sent to them (cf. Luke 24:27; John 2:22; 12:16; 14:26), and the words of the Scripture are regarded as living words of the Father of Jesus Christ (cf. John 6:44-46; Acts 3:17-26; Rom 1:1-6; 10:19-21; Heb 4:7; 1 Pet 2:6-10; 2 Pet 2:17).

1.1.3 Since, however, the Spirit (of the Father) of Jesus Christ not only fills the γραφαὶ ἅγιαι, but is also, and above all, manifested in the person and teaching of Jesus as well as in the witness of the apostles, the words of Jesus and the apostolic witness became, in time, the keys for understanding the Scriptures. Indications of this are found, for example, in the First Letter of Peter and in the Gospel of John.

1.1.3.1. According to 1 Pet 1:10-12, both the Old Testament prophets and the messengers who carry the Gospel are equally filled with the Holy Spirit. But the apostles are superior to the prophets, since they have the privilege of proclaiming his actual appearance and thus the fulfillment of the events which the prophets could only promise for the future (cf. the similar idea in Rom 1:1-6).

1.1.3.2 In the passion story of the Gospel of John we hear—as we do in the Synoptics (cf., e.g., Matt 27:9; Luke 22:37)—that the proclamations of the Scripture "are fulfilled" (cf. John 19:24, 28, 36, 37) in the suffering and death of Jesus. But the same verb (πληροῦσθαι) is used within the context of the same narrative with respect to the fulfillment of Jesus' prophecy of his own death.[6] According to John 18:8, Jesus reveals himself in Gethsemane to those who came to seize him and commands them to take only him, not his disciples, into custody "so that the words he had spoken would be fulfilled: 'I have not lost one of those you gave me'" (cf. John 6:39). In the same vein, we hear in John 18:32 that Pilate was pressured by Jewish opponents to execute Jesus "so that the words Jesus had spoken indicating the kind of death he was going to die would be fulfilled" (cf. John 3:14). These two parallel statements regarding fulfillment indicate clearly that in the school of John the prophecy of Jesus had gained the same authority as the γραφαί, which testify (only) to Jesus.

1.2 The tendency visible in these texts marks the beginning of a canonical process which overlaps the still continuing process of the formation (and translation) of the Old Testament. The words of Jesus as well as the teachings of the apostles are recorded and placed alongside the Holy Scriptures so that these could be interpreted in accordance with faith in Jesus Christ. Traces of this new canonical process can be seen as early as the middle of the first century.

1.2.1 As fundamental as the γραφαὶ ἅγιαι were for Paul, the Jesus-tradition and the apostolic testimony were also just as important. The apostle had a high regard for the "words of the Lord" (cf. 1 Cor 7:10), and he knows and teaches the Jesus-tradition (cf. 1 Cor 11:23-25). In 1 Cor 15:3-5 he quotes the "gospel" which he had learned himself and passed down to the Corinthians in the (baptismal) catechism. According to Rom 1:16, this Gospel is a "form of teaching" (τύπος διδαχῆς Rom 6:17) which is handed down to the Christians at baptism with the expectation that they be obedient to it. Paul, however, can also point out the spiritual quality of his own statements (cf. 1 Cor 7:40) and insist that his letters be exchanged between the various churches and be read before the whole congregation (cf. 1 Thess 5:27; Col 4:16).

1.2.2 As can be seen from the prologue of the Gospel of Luke, Luke 1:1-4, Luke the Evangelist writes his gospel narrative in order to expound the contents of the early Christian (baptismal) catechism which his patron of high position, Theophilus, had enjoyed. The commission of Jesus to become missionaries and to baptize in Matt 28:19-20 even requires that all the things which Jesus commanded his disciples were to be the subject of missionary teaching. This shows that the Gospel of Matthew was intended as a handbook for the mission to the Gentiles.

1.2.3 In John 21:24-25, the school of John furnishes its Fourth Gospel with the seal of a "true testimony," vouched for by the disciple whom Jesus loved, and at the end of Revelation all who would add to or subtract from the prophecy presented are threatened with the loss of their salvation (cf. Rev 22:18-19 with Deut 4:2;13:1).

1.3 The Second letter of Peter, which was probably (pseudepigraphically) written only after the turn of the century, already exhibits a considerable advancement in the canonical process over against the examples just mentioned: According to 2 Pet 3:15-16, a collection of "all" Paul's letters and "other books" (which possibly includes the Gospel of Matthew cited in 2 Pet 1:17) has already been placed alongside the inspired Holy Scriptures of the Old Testament (which are mentioned in 2 Pet 1:20-21). The author of the letter is of the opinion that all these books are to be interpreted in keeping with the apostolic faith so that they will not be misunderstood to support some heresy. *At this point, we stand before the beginnings of the two-part Christian canon, and we see that the New Testament itself has already constructed a concept for the appropriate interpretation of this canon!* [7]

> This concept is developed to counter Christian heretics who thought nothing (anymore) of expecting a parousia, and who held the common Christian teaching concerning the end times to be illusory (cf. 2 Pet 3:3-4). In the face of their criticism, "Peter" argues as follows: The voice of God, "this is my Son, whom I love; with him I am well pleased" (2 Pet 1:17, cf. the agreement with Matt 17:5 [and not with Mark 9:7; Luke 9:35]), which was called out with reference to Jesus as he himself, James and John were "with him on the sacred mountain," confirms with God's own words the prophetic word of Scripture from which it comes, i.e. Ps 2:7 (and Isa 42:1). According to Ps 2:7-8, the Son of God is to receive the nations as his inheritance and reign to the ends of the earth, and, according to Isa 42:1, the servant will bring God's justice to the nations. Thus, both verses speak of the Son of God being invested with the authority to rule. Furthermore, according to 2 Pet 1:20,

> the heretics, depending on their own critical interpretation (ἰδία ἐπίλυσις), fail to understand the inspired, prophetic word of the Scriptures, the Christological significance of which God himself (before the eyes and ears of the three apostles) had revealed. In contrast, those in the congregation who have been taught by the Apostles may hold fast to the expectation of the parousia, because they do not depend on their own interpretation in order to understand the prophecy of the Scriptures, but read and interpret it in accordance with the tradition to which the Apostles witness. They can also learn, according to 2 Pet 3:8-9, from Ps 90:4 (= "For a thousand years in your sight are like a day that has just gone by...") that God still refrains from the final judgment only because he, in his merciful patience, wants to give all humankind a chance to repent. Also, the letters of Paul (which, although in part difficult to understand, are still written with divine wisdom) witness to this patience of God (Rom 2:4; 3:25-26; 9:22-23; 11:11-12) if they are read in accord with the apostolic tradition, while "ignorant and unstable people distort" these statements of the apostle, "as they do the other Scriptures (τὰς λοιπὰς γραφάς), to their own destruction" (cf. 2 Pet 3:15-16). *The inspired prophecy of the Holy Scriptures and the letters of Paul (which are full of divine wisdom), as well as the remaining writings, are, thus, (only) correctly interpreted when they are understood in accordance with the apostolic tradition of faith.*

The canonical process has reached a similar state of advancement in 2 Peter as is present in Justin Martyr, who reports in Apol 1, 67 that the Roman congregation would read aloud on Sundays, along with the writings of the prophets, the "remembrances of the apostles," (τὰ ἀπομνημονεύματα τῶν ἀποστόλων), i.e. the Gospels, and that after that the principal would hold a sermon. Already in the first half of the second century CE, the γραφαὶ ἅγιαι, the Gospels, and the Letters of Paul all belong to the writings which the early Christian congregations regularly read aloud. Put in another way: the Old and New Testament Scriptures mentioned enjoy "canonical" authority.

1.4 If we follow the canonical process further, we find that the unity of the Old and New Testament was fundamentally called into question in only one instance in the early Church, namely, by Marcion and his followers in the middle of the second century. His rejection of the Old Testament could not assert itself in any of the other churches. Instead, the twofold question of these churches, which remained acute into the fourth century (and longer), was, which books should be included in the two-part Christian canon.

1.4.1 In the churches of the East, which had a closer connection to Judaism than those in the West, the twenty-two (22) books of the Hebrew canon were distinguished from the Apocrypha of the Septuagint. The former were declared a fixed part of the biblical canon, while the non-canonical Scriptures were judged to be only "school books" for the catechumens.[8] In the West, on the other hand, this distinction was not made and the Septuagint as a whole was accepted.[9]

1.4.2 As far as the New Testament is concerned, only one book in the East and one in the West caused problems, and in both instances because of the Montanists. The Revelation of John was controversial in the East because it encouraged the enthusiast tendencies of the heretics, and in the West Hebrews was troublesome because it (in Heb 6:4-8; 10:26-31) declared the so-called second repentance impossible and thus legitimized the ethical rigorism of the Montanists. But in the course of time, both books were eventually considered a part of the canon, despite misgivings.

1.5 The end result of the canonical process, in

which the formation of the (Hebrew) Old Testament, the translation and development of the Septuagint and the coming together of the New Testament are joined and overlap, is the two-part Christian Bible. It is considered holy by the churches because it bears witness to the unsurpassable revelation of the one God in and through Christ, which is the foundation of the Christian faith. Although the dispute over the position of the Apocrypha of the LXX has to this day not been settled,[10] there are no more serious ecclesiastical discussions concerning the central books of the Old and New Testament. Today, there is even agreement among Protestant and Catholic theologians over the statement that the churches did not simply create the Bible themselves, but that the biblical revelation was the motivating force of the canonical process. The Holy Bible which emerged out of this process must therefore retain its preeminence above all church doctrine.[11]

2. *The center of Scripture* [12]

Although the question concerning the theological center of Scripture has only been intensively discussed since the Reformation, it has been asked by the Church from the very beginning. The ancient church answered it by pointing to the so-called "rule of faith" (*regula fidei* or κανὼν τῆς πίστεως). This rule summarized the essential instructional content of the Bible in such a way that it could serve as an aid in learning the Christian faith. The Church has never been able to do without a clear and catechetically suitable summary of the main content of Scripture, and also today is unable to teach in accordance with the Scripture without it.[13]

2.1 Keeping this model of the ancient Church (and thus also the ecumenical model) found in the rule of faith in view,[14] we note that three modern variants in the discussion about "the center of Scripture" suffer from severe deficiencies:

2.1.1 First, there is the refusal to formulate a center of the Scripture at all, since all books of the Holy Scripture have the authority and deserve attention.[15] If one clings to this principle, one avoids the duty of the Church to advocate a faith doctrine which is well-founded biblically. Furthermore one ignores the fact that the two-part Christian canon includes main books and secondary books, the contents of which differ in significance.

2.1.2 Then, there is the attempt to formulate one center for the Old Testament and another for the New, while pointing out that the Old Testament not only represents a preliminary stage to the New, but is to be given due consideration apart from it.[16] Such a procedure, however, overlooks the fact that the Old and New Testaments stem from one complex canonical process. One also fails to take sufficient note of the problems which arise when one attempts to piece together the act of salvation of the one God in and through his only Son in the Holy Spirit, of which the Bible testifies, from independent Old and New Testament partial elements.

2.1.3 Finally, it is not legitimate to reduce the center of scripture down to (genuine) Paulinism.[17] Although this may appear to be in the spirit of the Reformation, this reduction stands contrary to the understanding of Scripture espoused by LUTHER and the reformers, who never suggested an isolated esteem only for the letters of Paul (and especially not just for certain parts of them).[18] The teachings of Paul are biblically incomparable in their theological precision, but they cannot, nor do they want to be, uncoupled from the Old Testament, nor should they be isolated from nor made absolute over against the testimony of the other central books of the New Testament.

If one attempts to avoid the three mistakes mentioned, then one must make certain when formulating a center of the Scripture that the statements satisfy two requirements: They must be comprehensive enough to do justice to the witness of the main writings of the Old and New Testaments, but must also be sufficiently exact to answer the fundamental soteriological question concerning what event is responsible for faith in Jesus Christ and what people have to contribute to their salvation at the end of time and what not, a question which was already controversial within the Bible (and has remained so in the Church).

If one attempts to make a statement with regard to content, one may say the following: The one God who created the world and chose Israel to be his own people has through the sending, the work, and the death and resurrection of his only Son, Jesus Christ, sufficiently provided once and for all for the salvation of Jews and Gentiles. Jesus Christ is the hope of all creation. Whoever believes in him as Reconciler and Lord and obeys his instruction maybe certain of their participation in the kingdom of God. Among the biblical texts to be mentioned which witness to this center are, naturally, first and foremost those from the New Testament: John 11:25-26; 14:6; 1 John 2:1-2; 4:9-10; Rom 1:1-6; 1:16-17 + 3:21-31; 1 Tim 2:5-6 etc. But these texts belong inextricably with Old Testament texts such as Ex 20:1-6; Deut 6:4-5; Hos 11:8-9; Isa 7:9; 9:5-6; 25:6-9; 43:1-7; Isa 52:13-53:12; Jer 31:31-34; Ps 139:1-16; Prov 8:22-36 etc., because without this Old Testament foundation the statements of the New Testament remain incomplete and subject to misinterpretation.

2.3 The insight that the Bible has only one center makes it possible to relate the biblical witness to this center in a differentiating manner. Viewing things from this center, we realize not only that the Old and New Testament confess the triune God, but that the biblical books divide themselves into central and secondary writings with respect to this center. Futhermore, this center makes it possible to differentiate between the indirect witness to Christ in the Old Testament and the direct witness in the New, between gospel and law, blessing and curse, belief and unbelief.

3. *The Interpretation of Holy Scriptures*

3. Critical for the interpretation of the Holy Scriptures is that a fundamental hermeneutic principle be consistently followed. This principle has been formulated by HARTMUT GESE for the exegesis of biblical texts as follows: "A text should be understood in the way that it wants to be understood, i.e. as it understands itself."[19] Since the texts of the Bible want to be understood as inspired witnesses (see below), the *biblical way to knowledge,* to which both Old and New Testaments testify, must be accorded due attention when interpreting them.[20]

3.1 This way runs through two poles. The first pole is represented by Israel's "theory of cognition *in nuce*,"[21] Proverbs 1:7: "The fear of the Lord is the beginning of knowledge." The mystery of God delimits and is the foundation of all human knowledge of truth; each person may and should allow this mystery to be supplied to him or her in order that one might come to know oneself, the world, and God. The second pole is represented by Gal 4:9 and 1 Cor 13:12: God's knowledge of humanity precedes all of humanity's knowledge of God. The human being can only know God and his ways to the extent that God reveals himself to each human being. The deciding test-case for this is biblical revelation (cf. Isa 6:1-10; Bar 3:37; Matt 11:27; 2 Cor 4:1-6; 1 Cor 12:3; John 6:67-69): The recognition of the truth of this revelation can only be made accessible and be freely given by God. Following Ezek 36:25-27; Jer 31:31-34; John 16:13 and 1 Cor 2:16, one can also say: Recognition of revelation is a knowledge which is only accessible through the Holy Spirit and which includes a life with and in this truth. The hermeneutical implications of this can be summarized in one sentence: One can only fathom the truth of the biblical texts and penetrate to the center of Scripture when one pays attention to the biblical way to knowledge and takes due account of the fact that these texts want to communicate, above all, (revelatory) wisdom, the truth of which can only be fully gauged when it is accepted and integrated into one's own life (cf. John 7:16-17).

3.2 We have already shown that the New Testament authors considered the "Holy Scriptures" inspired and interpreted them in the spirit of the faith (cf. 2 Tim 3:16; 2 Pet 1:20-21). In the New Testament this view of inspiration was already extended to include the witness of Jesus and the apostles. A good example of why and how this happened can be seen in the Johannine doctrine of the Spirit-Paraclete, in 1 Cor 2:6-16, and in 2 Peter.

According to John 14:26; 16:13-15, the preaching and work of Jesus were truly understood for the first time as they were brought to remembrance by the "Spirit of truth," which Jesus sent after he had left to return to his Father. John 21:24-25 suggest that the whole Gospel of John wants to be understood as the expression of such a knowledge effected by the Spirit. The prophecy of Revelation, too, is considered a gift of God, communicated by the Spirit (Rev 1:1,10), and for this reason it is forbidden to add to or take anything away from the book (cf. the Rev 22:18-20).—Independent from John, Paul presents a hermeneutical model in 1 Cor 2:6-16 which points to the inspiration of the apostolic witnesses: While the Jewish leaders did not recognize who Jesus was and therefore brought the "Lord of glory" to the cross (cf. Acts 3:17; 13:27), the Apostle (after his calling) was allowed through the gift of the Spirit to recognize who Jesus in truth was and understand that the cross signified God's eschatological act of salvation in and through Christ. By interpreting these spiritual things to spiritual people in Corinth with words taught by the Spirit (1 Cor 2:13-14), Paul transmits to them the revealed knowledge which he had been given, and they cannot be understood by the readers other than through the Spirit.[22]—The Second Letter of Peter assumes not only the inspiration of the Old Testament prophecy (cf. 1:21), but also that the letters of Paul are filled with divine wis-

> dom[23] (cf. 3:15-16). Furthermore, it shows that, on the basis of this view, criteria had been developed for the correct interpretation of inspired Scriptures (see 58f.).

3.3 *According to the New Testament, then, the Holy Scriptures which point to Christ, the Jesus-tradition, and the apostolic witness can only be appropriately interpreted when the exegetes participate in the Spirit which prevails throughout in these traditions, and their interpretation can only be heard with understanding when the Spirit discloses the meaning to the hearer.* Thus, all interpretation of Scripture, which truly intends to interpret the Scriptures in the way in which they want to be interpreted, is done under the condition that only God himself, through Christ and in the power of the Holy Spirit, can engender an understanding of Scripture. For the New Testament authors, the natural environment for such biblical interpretation is the Church of Jesus Christ, which is filled with the Spirit (cf. 1 Cor 14:24-25; Eph 2:19-22; 4:4).

3.4 Since these things have long been recognized and considered, all ecclesiastical hermeneutics have, since the days of the ancient Church, proceeded from the principle: "The Holy Scripture must be read and interpreted in the spirit in which it was written."[24] This principle was also accepted by LUTHER and the reformers.[25]

3.5 An exegesis which is really sympathetic to the biblical texts and which is suited to them has not only the duty to bring attention to these hermeneutic criteria which have been provided by the Bible, but also must make an attempt to adhere to them. If one tries to do this, then a biblical hermeneutic cannot only, nor primarily, address the question of how we are to understand the Bible today and how we can appropriate its message. Before one can deal with the question of appropriation, it must be made clear that the Holy Scripture itself has developed criteria which show how it is to be interpreted as a whole and in individual texts: The spirit-filled texts of the Scripture want to be interpreted in the Spirit.

3.5.1 With respect to method, this means that the usual ensemble of historical methods and the critical suspicion over against all historical material which guides them is not adequate to discover the truth of the biblical faith message. Historical criticism represents an important (and, in my opinion, essential) tool only for penetrating the historical dimension of the individual texts and the collective traditions of the Bible. The work done with this tool must be paired with the willingness to allow oneself to be confronted with the mystery of God in the biblical traditions (cf. Prov 1:7), and this willingness springs from the expectation that God does in fact reveal himself through Scripture (cf. Gal 4:9).[26]

3.5.2 If one works with the biblical text within this framework, then the analytical results of the interpretation are not the only thing nor the last word that biblical exegesis has to say; it may and must go beyond the dimension of historical statements and become a witness to the truth itself. Only when it speaks, also with respect to content, of the revelation of the one God in and through Christ and subjects itself to this revelation, can the theological exegesis of Scripture gather up people upon the way which God has gone in and through Christ in order that He might lead them to faith and salvation.[27]

3.6 Under these circumstances, the Christian interpretation of the Bible presents itself as a task which can be accomplished neither by Old and New Testament exegetes nor by theological scholarship alone. It is the task of the whole (ecumenical) Church. This task can only be undertaken with the understanding that the biblical word of God, in the power of its own authority, makes itself heard even before theology begins her work, and that it does not stop making itself heard when her work is through.[28] The scholarly exegesis of the Old and New Testaments has, within the circle of all theological disciplines, only the special task of being an advocate for the texts, discovering the original historical meaning, and protecting them against (all possible types of) instrumental misuse. But when confronted with the Holy Scriptures, which interpret themselves, all scholarly exegetes, together with the whole theological community and all Christians, remain nothing other than beggars dependent on God's gifts.[29]

NOTES

1. Translation from the Revised Standard Version.

2. For the apocryphal tradition in 1 Cor 2:9 cf. H. P. RÜGER, "Das Werden des christlichen Alten Testaments," *JBTh* 3, (1988) 175-189 (esp. 178).

3. These "border-line" texts, however, are not at all unimportant in understanding the New Testament! On the contrary, they paved the way for a sapiential understanding of Christology (e.g. in Col 1:1-20; John 1:1-18), and without them it would be difficult, if not impossible, to explain how the divine title "Lord of Glory" from 1 Enoch 22:14; 63:2 came to be applied to Christ in 1 Cor 2:8. Also the title "Son of Man" applied to Jesus would remain unintelligible without Dan 7, and the so-called book of the Similitudes in the Ethiopic Apocalypse of Enoch, 1 Enoch 37-71 (cf. 1 Enoch 46:1-3; 48:2; 62:5-6, 9, 14; 63:11). Cf. my article, "The Significance of the Old Testament Apocrypha and Pseudepigrapha for the Understanding of Jesus and Christology," in *The Apocrypha in Ecumenical Perspective*, United Bible Societies Monograph Series No. 6, ed. S. MEURER, 1991, pp. 1-15. (Originally "Die Bedeutung der Apokryphen und Pseudepigraphen des Alten Testaments für das Verständnis Jesu und der Christologie," in Die *Apokryphernfrage im ökumenischen Horizont*, Die Bibel in der Welt, Bd. 22, ed. S. MEURER, 1989, pp. 13-25.)

4. Cf. L. GOPPELT, *Typos, The Typological Interpretation of the Old Testament in the New* (1939), ET 1882.

5. Cf. (H. STRACK-)P. BILLERBECK, *Kommentar zum Neuen Testament*, vol. 4, 1964[4], pp. 443-451. If one wants to be more specific, one must assume that the New Testament followed early Judaism in believing in the so called personal inspiration of the biblical authors. As H. BURKHARDT, *Die Inspiration heiliger Schriften bei Phi-*

lo von Alexandrien, 1988, has convincingly shown, Philo of Alexandria also subscribed to this view. One should, therefore, no longer make a distinction between a Palestinian idea of inspiration and a Hellenistic one, as did, for example, J. JEREMIAS when he wrote, "... while in Palestine one still held that the human tools of God made a contribution, the Diaspora (Philo) tended towards a rigid verbal inspiration, in which they were only involuntary stylies of the Spirit" *(Die Briefe an Timotheus und Titus*, 1981[12/2], p. 62), but one should posit a single view of inspiration within early Judaism which early Christianity then adopted.

6. This observation was made by late colleague H. P. RÜGER in a manuscript which has unfortunately remained unpublished.

7. Cf. for this my book *Vom Verstehen des Neuen Testaments*, 1986[2], pp. 54f. pp. 75f.

8. So in the 39th Easter Letter of Athanasius from the year 367, cf. the excerpts in PREUSCHEN ANALECTA, 1910[2], pp. 42-45. For an English translation see P. SCHAFF and M. WACE (eds.) *Nicene and Post-Nicene Fathers*, Second Series 1-4, Grands Rapids 1955 (1890- 99), vol. 4, pp. 551ff.

9. Cf. the rescript of Pope Innocence I to the Bishop of Toulouse from the year 405, in which the names of all Old and New Testament writings are named without differentiating between canonical and Apocryphal books (For the text see DENZINGER-SCHÖNMETZER, Nr. 213).

10. Cf. the report by H. P. RÜGER, "Der Umfang des alttestamentlichen Kanons in den verschiedenen kirchlichen Traditionen," in *Die Apokryphenfrage* (see n. 3), pp. 137-145.

11. Cf. the amazing joint declaration of the ecumenical committee of Protestant and Catholic theologians, "Kanon—Heilige Schrift —Tradition," in *Verbindliches Zeugnis* (eds.) W. PANNENBERG and T. SCHNEIDER, 1992, pp. 37-397.

12. For the following, cf. my article, "Die Mitte der Schrift—biblisch—theologisch betrachtet," in *Wissenschaft und Kirche*, FS für E. Lohse, (eds.) K. ALAND and S. MEURER, 1989, pp. 29-56.

13. Cf. K. BEYSCHLAG, *Grundriss der Dogmengeschichte*, vol. 1, 1982, pp. 149-172.

14. K. BEYSCHLAG, cites ibid (see n. 13), p. 155, Tertullian, *De praescr. 13* as an example: "The rule of faith is that rule ... according to which one believes that there exists only one creator of the world and none other beside him, that he brought everything into existence from nothing through his 'Word' which proceeded (from him) before all things, that this 'Word'—called his Son—seen in the name of God by the patriarchs in various ways, ever perceived in the prophets, finally descended from the Spirit and power of the Father into the virgin Mary, took on flesh in her womb and was born as Jesus Christ, that he then proclaimed the new law and the new promise of the kingdom of

God, performed miracles, was nailed to the cross, rose from the dead on the third day, was taken up into heaven and took his place at the right hand of God—to take his place he sent the power of the Holy Spirit, who leads the believers—that he will return in glory to gather up the holy ones that they might enjoy eternal life and the promise of heaven, and will condemn the godless to eternal fire, after both groups (holy and godless) have been raised from the dead and their bodies restored." (English translation based on the German by K. Beyschlag.)

15. Cf. for example, G. Maier, *Biblische Hermeneutik*, 1990, pp. 174-178.

16. Cf. B. S. CHILDS, "Biblische Theologie und christlicher Kanon," *JBTH* 3 (1988) pp.13-27, and his *Biblical Theology of the Old and New Testaments*, 1992.

17. Cf. S. SCHULTZ, *Die Mitte der Schrift*, 1976.

18. For confirmation, one need only look to LUTHER's statement regarding the question, "Welches die rechten und edelsten Bücher des Neuen Testaments sind," which conclude his *Vorrede* to the *Septembertestament* from 1522. For the texts cf. *Luthers Vorreden zur Bibel*, (ed.) H. BORNKAMM, 1967, pp. 140f.

19. "Hermeneutische Grundsätze der Exegese biblischer Texte," in H. GESE, *Alttestamentliche Studien*, 1991, pp. 249-264, (esp. p. 249).

20. Cf. H. DIEM, *Ja oder Nein*, 1974, pp. 282-290.

21. G. v. RAD, *Weisheit in Israel*, 1970, p. 94.

22. Cf. my article, "The Hermeneutical Significance of 1 Cor 2:6-16," in *Tradition and Interpretation in the New Testament. Essays in Honor of E. Earle Ellis for His 60th Birthday*, (eds.) G. F. HAWTHORNE with O. BETZ, 1987, pp. 328-347. (Originally "Zur hermeneutischen Bedeutung von 1 Kor 2:6-16," *TheolBeitr* 18, [1987] pp. 133-158.)

23. The endowment with wisdom is a mode of inspiration, cf. Sir 39:6 (and 24:30-34).

24. Dei Verbum III, 12; this principle is attributed to Jerome in Gal 5:19-21. Migne PL 26, 445 A.

25. LUTHER writes in his "Assertio omnium articulorum M. Lutheri per bullam Leonis X novissimam damnatorum" from 1520: "I do not want to be praised as he who is more scholarly than all others; rather, I want the Scripture alone to be the queen. Furthermore, I do not want the Scripture to be interpreted through my own spirit or from the spirit of another person, but that it *be understood through itself and through its own spirit* (WA 7:98,40-99,2. The English translation here is based on the German translation of E. HIRSCH, *Hilfsbuch zum Studium der Dogmatik*, 4th Ed., 1964, p. 85).

26. Cf. K. BARTH, *Einführung in die evangelische Theologie*, 1963,[2] pp. 193f.: "The discipline of Biblical Theology does not operate…in a vacuum, but in service to the Church of Jesus Christ, which is

established by the prophetic-apostolic witness. For this reason she approaches these texts in the expectation—more should not be said, but also not less!—that this witness will be encountered in them, while, at the same time, she must of course (and this is what is meant by the so-called 'hermeneutical circle') remain completely open to the question of whether, to what extent, in which way and in which concrete statements this expectation is fulfilled, or the status which these texts have for the Church is confirmed. 'Dogmatic' exegesis? She is that only in as far as she rejects any dogma which would want to disallow this expectation from the very beginning and to declare fulfillment of this expectation for impossible from the very beginning. 'Pneumatic' exegesis? Surely not, if she thinks she could lord over the texts through some supposed personal possession of the Spirit. She could, however, be named such when she takes hold of the freedom (a freedom which is to be anchored in the Scripture itself) seriously, finally, and decisively to question the texts only regarding the testimony of the Spirit to itself, which can be experienced in these texts."

27. Cf. my article: "Geistliche Schriftauslegung?" in *Einfach vor Gott reden, FS für F. Mildenberger zum 65. Geburtstag,* (eds.) J. ROLOFF and H. G. ULRICH, 1994, pp. 67-81.

28. F. MILDENBERGER uses an illuminating formulation in describing the relationship of the scholarly theology and exegesis to the ever-continuing self-interpretation of the Scriptures. He writes that theological scholarship must critically accompany the "elementary talk about God" (German: *einfache Gottesrede);* cf. his *Biblische Dogmatik,* vol. 1, 1991, pp. 11 and 30.

29. Cf. Luther's last note, WA, TR 5; 318,2 (no. 5677).

5

SUMMARY AND OVERVIEW

1. *The State of Biblical Theology*

The large and well-known Theologies of the Old and New Testament with which we work today were published between 1953 and 1976. In 1953, the famous "Theologie des Neuen Testaments" by RUDOLF BULTMANN, which appeared in three fascicles, was completed. A student of BULTMANN, HANS CONZELMANN, published his *Grundriss der Theologie des Neuen Testaments* (ET *An Outline of the Theology of the New Testament*, 1969) in 1964. In 1969 appeared *Die Theologie des Neuen Testaments nach seinen Hauptzeugen* (ET *The Theology of the New Testament According to its Major Witnesses*, 1973) from WERNER GEORG KÜMMEL. Printed in 1971 was the first (and only) volume of the *Neutestamentliche Theologie* (ET 1971) from JOACHIM JEREMIAS, the subject of which was the proclamation of Jesus. *A Theology of the New Testament* from GEORGE ELDON LADD appeared in 1974, as did EDUARD LOHSE's *Grundriss neutestamentlicher Theologie*. In 1975/76, JÜRGEN ROLOFF published posthumously the *Theologie des Neuen Testaments* of his teacher, LEONARD GOPPELT, and between 1968 and 1976 the four-volume *Theologie des Neuen Testaments* from KARL HERMANN SCHELKLE appeared. All of these works document how a famous generation of scholars understood the New Testament theologically, and they are in use to this day (in reprints and new editions), and justifiably so.

Since 1990, new comprehensive publications have again begun to appear on this subject, and they will become *nolens volens* (whether they want to or not) documents of the theological understanding of the New Testament which the generation which studied under the authors just mentioned has achieved. This generation, however, is strongly influenced by KARL BARTH and has also learned from such famous Old Testament scholars as GERHARD VON RAD, HANS WALTER WOLF and WALTHER ZIMMERLI. They transmitted to their students the desire that one day the exegetes of the Old and New Testaments would take up the challenge to once again work out a *Biblical Theology which includes both testaments*. For this reason, an issue has been pushed into the forefront for this new generation of scholars which had only been incidentally treated in the theologies of their teachers: the significance of the Old Testament for the New Testament and the relation of both Testaments to one another in the Christian Bible. Meanwhile, three theologies have recently been published which tackle exactly this topic: The *Biblical Theology of the Old and New Testaments* by the Old Testament scholar at Yale, BREVARD S. CHILDS, the three-volume *Biblische Theologie des Neuen Testaments* by the New Testament scholar HANS HÜBNER in Göttingen, and my own of the same title, to appear in two volumes.

1.1 The book by BREVARD S. CHILDS, published in 1992, represents the mature summation of a life's work devoted to the theological interpretation of the Old and New Testaments in their canonical form and in canonical context. CHILDS, whose theology is strongly influenced by that of WALTER ZIMMERLI, has ventured to construct a Biblical Theology of both testaments. With great theological competence and an admirable breadth of knowledge of theological literature, he treats four problem-complexes one after the other: First, fundamental questions of Biblical Theology, then the discrete witness of the Old Testament, followed by the discrete witness of the New Testament, and finally, the theological doctrines of God, his covenant, Christ, reconciliation, law and gospel, humanity, faith, the kingdom of God and ethics which result from both testaments.

1.1.1 CHILDS proceeds in this manner because, according to his view, the two-part Christian canon, made up of the Old and New Testaments, was formed in the following historical stages: After the large Old Testament corpora of tradition had already had a centuries long canonical process behind them, they were gathered together from the fourth century BCE on into the canon of the Hebrew Bible, consisting of the Torah, Prophets, and Writings. It was already completed by the second century BCE and was also gradually translated into Greek, during which process the Hebrew text always retained a normative authority above the Greek. The Septuagint, which was produced by this translation process, does not, therefore, have the same canonical quality as the Hebrew canon. After a period between the testaments of around 200 years, the events of Easter in the first half of the first century CE mark the beginning of the formation of New Testament tradition, which then goes through its own canonical process of one hundred or more years. It is driven by two motivating factors: the great significance of the Christ-event and the light which the Holy Scriptures (of the Old Testament) throw upon this event when they are interpreted Christologically. While Judaism rejected the Septuagint after the failure of both revolts against Rome and definitively fixed the Hebrew Bible, the ancient Church took up the twofold impulse of the New Testament formation of tradition, binding together the writings of the Hebrew Bible with the twenty-seven (27) books of the New Testament to form the two-part Christian canon. In the East, the so-called Old Testament Apocrypha were excluded from the canon, while in the West they were included.

1.1.2 Anyone who is not satisfied with analyzing

this canon only in a historical critical fashion (and thus subjectively), but desires to interpret it theologically as well, must, according to CHILDS, follow the canonical textual form of the biblical books as well as the order in which they appear in the canon. Furthermore, after treating the Old and New Testaments as independent witnesses, the teachings of both testaments must be taken together in order to produce a fundamental outline of a Christian biblical dogmatic. CHILDS follows all of these steps himself, and one can only hope that his profound work finds many reflective readers who allow themselves to be guided by him to a theological interpretation of the Holy Scripture, taken in its entirety.

1.2 Two volumes of the *Biblische Theologie des Neuen Testaments* being written by HANS HÜBNER have appeared to date. The first appeared in 1990 and, carrying the title "Prolegomena," thoroughly deals with the fundamental theological problems of a Biblical Theology. The second volume came out in 1993 and discusses the theology of Paul and the history of its influence in the New Testament. This, for Hübner, is the heart of a Biblical Theology of the New Testament. The third volume, which is still to come, is intended to deal with the remaining New Testament witnesses and systematically sum up the whole work. It has already become obvious that HÜBNER's Biblical Theology differs fundamentally from CHILDS'. HÜBNER only treats the New Testament, chooses a different starting point, assesses the value of the Septuagint differently, and pursues a different goal of theological interpretation.

1.2.1 The decisive *starting point* of a Biblical Theology of the New Testament lies for HÜBNER in the many quotations from and allusions to the Old Testament which are woven into the fabric of many of the New Testament books. Since only a selection of Old Testament texts are interpreted in the quotations and allusions, he differentiates between the "Vetus Testamentum in Novo Receptum" and the "Vetus Testamentum per se". He is thus able to distinguish the Hebrew Bible from its only partial assimilation by the Christians, and, proceeding from here, he can question critically whether, and if so, how the God of the Hebrew Bible is also the God of the New Testament. With his procedure, HÜBNER opposes CHILDS' "canonical approach," but must also submit to two (in my opinion decisive) objections from him. According to CHILDS, making the quotations and allusions the starting point does not produce a deep and comprehensive enough understanding of the relation between the testaments.[1] Furthermore a differentiating between an Old Testament assimilated into the New and the Old Testament alone is theologically unacceptable because it critically passes by the Old and New Testament witness to the work and will of the one God (cf. Ex 3:14; Deut 6:4; Rom 3:30).[2] Both objections are in my opinion legitimate.

1.2.2 With respect to the Septuagint, HÜBNER makes the historically correct point that the importance of the Septuagint for ancient Judaism and early Christianity can hardly be overestimated. According to him, it plays a much greater role in the question concerning the relation of the two testaments than CHILDS (representative for many Old Testament scholars) thinks.[3] If one accepts Hübner's objection, then the picture CHILDS sketches of the canonical process has to undergo fundamental revision. The Septuagint came into existence at a time when only the Torah and the Prophets had canonical status, while the third part of the Hebrew canon was still in formation. The development of the Septuagint, which lasted from the third century BCE to the second century CE, was a complex process of translation, of revision of the translation on the basis of the Hebrew texts, and of increasing the number of translated writings by adding Hellenistic-Jewish writings of instruction and edification (such as the Wisdom of Solomon and the books of the Maccabees).[4] Since the final canonical form of the Hebrew Bible was not achieved until the end of the first and beginning of the second century CE, the translation of the Septuagint lasted at least this long, the so-called apocryphal books of the Septuagint were of great importance for the formation of the New Testament witness to Christ, and the Septuagint was never canonized apart from the New Testament writings, *one must speak of one canonical process from which the Hebrew Bible, the Septuagint, and the New Testament all proceed and which, although multi-layered, represents a continuum.* This common process renders the discussion about a long intertestamental period unnecessary and the distinction between a discrete witness of the Old Testament and one of the New Testament highly questionable. In other words, if one gives due attention to the historical role which the Septuagint has played in ancient Judaism and early Christianity and takes into consideration the complex data of the history of the canon, then it becomes clear that CHILDS, in the writing of his work, has followed a picture of the formation of the Hebrew and Christian Bible which is no less artificially construed than HÜBNER's differentiation between the "Vetus Testamentum per se" and the "Vetus Testamentum in Novo Receptum".

1.2.3 The theological goal of HÜBNER's interpretation lies in a biblical theological renewal of the existential interpretation of RUDOLF BULTMANN. In order to achieve this goal, he must, in the course of his exegetical-historical work, immediately combine his historical reconstruction with the question of its meaning and intelligibility for the modern reader and throw those New Testament texts into relief which meet these requirements. This is why HÜBNER in the second volume of his work explicates, above all, Paul's discovery and development of the doctrine of justification and points out its existential significance for people (today). The existential interpretation determines Hübner work to such a degree that he forgoes showing in any historical detail how the apostle and his school understood God's act of reconciliation in and through Christ and the eschatological event of justification as well as the conception of creation and redemption into which they were embedded. In contrast to CHILDS, his theology will therefore in all probability contain no detailed outline of a Biblical Dogmatics, but only a doctrine of faith in Jesus Christ which emphasizes the theology of justification and is, furthermore, based only on Pauline (and certainly also Johannine) texts.

1.2.4 In view of the enormous biblical theological (and hermeneutical) deficiencies of the existential interpretation, which have been pointed out often enough in the past thirty years,[5] it must be feared that HÜBNER's concept will only be able to provide a very relative advance in understanding beyond Bultmann. The intention of his interpretation takes away by its very design all possibilities of any substantially new biblical understanding which a canonical approach to the Bible offers. Furthermore, in making "Vetus Testamentum in Novo Receptum" his point of departure, he is confronted with a highly problematical central question, i.e., "whether in fact the Jahwe of Israel, the national God of this people, is identical with the Father of Jesus Christ, the God of all humanity."[6] Whoever asks such a question can, even with a positive answer, hardly consider the Old Testament to be anything other than merely a (religio-) historical preliminary stage to the New, the significance and worth of which will only be decided on the basis of the New Testament revelation. Indeed, years ago, G. VON RAD, H. W. WOLFF, W. ZIMMERLI, and other leading Old Testament scholars rose up in protest against this undervaluation of the Old Testament, and CHILDS insists again in his work that the Old Testament and its testimony is not just a preliminary stage, but is and remains an essential part of the two-part Christian canon. In view of Jesus (cf. Luke 11:2/Matt 6:9; Luke 10:21-22/Matt 11:25-27), Paul (Rom 4:3-5, 17, 24-25), and John (cf. John 1:17-18), Hübner's vexing question should be rejected in favor of the position of these Old Testament scholars.

1.3. If we are to make progress, we must begin differently than HÜBNER and accept the risk involved in leaving the beaten tracks of the conventional exegesis of the Old and New Testament when we find that they lead us historically, and thus theologically, astray. I am attempting with *my* Biblical Theology of the New Testament (vol.1: 1992) to strike out upon this way and am well aware of the risk of such an endeavor.[7] Three fundamental determinations characterize this path.

1.3.1 Whoever wants to penetrate the texts of the Bible theologically and reach their core of truth must interpret them in the way in which they themselves demand to be interpreted and be prepared to tailor their method of interpretation to fit the individual character and individual significance of the texts.[8] In this way, the conventional historical critical treatment of the text is, in a certain sense, turned completely around. Classical historical criticism is guided by a methodical doubt with regard to the transmitted traditions and analyzes them with the intention of allowing only that to stand as truth which meets a modern definition of such. But biblical exegesis is confronted with a tradition which, according to ancient church experience, claims to witness to the unsurpassable truth of the revelation of God in and through Christ in words which are completely human but inspired by the Holy Spirit. Although it is true that an interpretation can only do justice to this claim to truth when it attempts to gain insight into the historical dimension of the text using all the tools of the critical trade, it must, at the same time, be prepared to champion the biblical maxim (one could indeed say cognitive theory!) of Prov 1:7: "The fear of the Lord is the beginning of knowledge." Put another way, *the theological exegesis of the Holy Scriptures may and must allow itself to be confronted with the mystery of God's work for humanity in and through Christ. In so far as it is ready to accept this requirement, it has—as has all theology indebted to KARL BARTH—to quote the fitting words of ERNST FUCHS, "been given the honor of joining with God on his path to humanity and gathering up people upon that path."*[9]

1.3.2 The relationship between both testaments in the Christian Bible is determined by two factors. First, the fact that Jesus and the apostles chosen by him, as well as Paul, were born Jews, provided Christianity with a permanent part in "the Holy Scriptures" (of the Old Testament). Second, the complexity of the canonical process which produced both the Hebrew Old Testament, the Septuagint and the New Testament (see above) must be recognized. The process ends with the formation of the two-part Christian canon in the fourth century CE. *The theological center of this canon is the witness to God's act of salvation for Jews and Gentiles in and through Christ. This witness has Old and New Testament roots, but it is an inseparable, unified whole, because the one God, who created the world and chose Israel to be his own people, achieved once and for all in his only begotten Son, Jesus Christ, salvation for the world.*

1.3.3 It is this witness which determines the task of a Biblical Theology of the New Testament *which may and should show the way of God to humanity in and through Christ on the basis of the New Testament texts.* This way begins with the creation, runs through the complete history of Israel's election, reaches its apex in the sending, passion and resurrection of Jesus, and leads further to the kingdom of God, which the exalted Christ is to (and will) establish. The concrete historical reproduction of the apostolic witnesses to this way is possible only when one not only investigates the citations from and allusions to the Old Testament books in the New Testament, but also illuminates the points of reference between the traditions of the two testaments, including the shared language and common conceptual world. Furthermore, it requires an exact as possible reconstruction, based on the Gospels, of the sending of Jesus, his passion and resurrection, a thorough presentation of the origin and development of the proclamation of Christ by the (central) witnesses of the New Testament, and must be rounded off with a sketch of the formation of the two-part Christian canon and an investigation of its theological significance for the Church. Since scholarly biblical exegesis takes up its place within the context formed by all theological disciplines, it must, above all, be an advocate for the biblical texts as they appear in the biblical canon. It may and must repeat the testimony of these texts and give a theological summary of them, but need not take over the task of dogmatic theology as well.

Therefore, it should also refrain from trying to explain the meaning of the biblical witness for the present with an independent existential-analytical program, while for the most part ignoring the whole history of interpretation of the Holy Scriptures and complex dogmatic questions.

2. *The contents of a Biblical Theology*[10]

In attempting to realize these principles, those working in the field of New Testament should limit their efforts to developing a Biblical Theology of the New Testament which is open to the Old Testament, while at the same time hoping that a Biblical Theology of the Old Testament will be developed which is open to the New Testament. A single author is hardly in a position to be conversant with the current state of scholarly discussion in both Old and New Testament disciplines, and the wider the field of study is that one chooses, the more dilettantish are one's judgments in many matters. This is certainly not beneficial in accomplishing the task at hand.

2.1 A Biblical Theology of the New Testament must begin with a description of the preaching of Jesus according to the testimony of the Synoptics, because in this way it becomes clear that Christian faith is founded on the salvation act of the one God in the sending, work, passion, and resurrection of Jesus of Nazareth which precedes all faith (cf. Rom 5:6-8).

2.1.1 In the last thirty years, such scholars as E. EARLE ELLIS, BIRGER GERHARDSSON, MARTIN HENGEL, HEINZ SCHÜRMANN, and RAINER RIESNER have shown that the witness of the Synoptic Gospels is based on a school tradition which Jesus himself founded, was carefully preserved by the disciples, or pupils (μαθηταί), of Jesus, and handed down to the early church, the core members of which were at the beginning these same μαθηταί (Acts 1:13-14). Because of this continuum of traditions and of people, the synoptic material is historically much more reliable than often assumed. *The earthly Jesus and the Christ to which this tradition witnesses are almost exactly one and the same.*

2.1.2 The Gospel of Mark in Mark 1:1 bears witness to Jesus Christ as the "Son of God." This is by all means congruent with the earthly existence and intention of Jesus, who considered himself, according to Luke 10:21-22/Matt 11:25-25, the "Son" of his Heavenly Father. The Marcan passion-story clearly indicates that Jesus was condemned and crucified because of his claim to be the messianic Son of God (cf. Mark 14:61-62 par.). He accepted his violent death, knowing for certain that he was the messianic servant sent from God who was to provide with his life, once and for all, atonement for Israel (and the nations). As an analysis of Mark 10:45 and 14:24 par. shows, the words of God in Isa 43:3-4 and 52:13-53:12 led Jesus to this understanding of his death. The discovery of the empty tomb and the appearances of Jesus from heaven before "the witnesses chosen by God" (Acts 10:41) led Peter and the other disciples of Jesus to the revolutionary recognition that God had raised Jesus from the dead and made him "both Lord and Christ" (Acts 2:35). They then established the first church in Jerusalem, collected the Jesus-tradition there, and thus laid the foundation for the historical witness which has come down to us in the form of the Synoptic Gospels.

2.2 The *testimony of the apostle Paul* is of especially great significance for a Biblical Theology.

2.2.1 The key to the proclamation and theology of Paul lies in the calling of this persecutor of Christians to become an apostle of Jesus Christ on the road to Damascus (cf. Gal 1:1,15-16; 2 Cor 4:5-6; Rom 1:1-5). This event forced Paul to recognize three things, namely, that the crucified Jesus "was declared the Son of God in power by his resurrection" by God himself (cf. Rom 1:4), that Paul himself—because he, in his militant zeal for the law (cf. Gal 1:14), had persecuted the young Church of Jesus Christ—had fundamentally rebelled against God's plans for salvation, and, furthermore, that, despite this, he had been shown mercy and been given the privilege as an apostle of Jesus Christ to preach the Gospel of Christ (cf. 1 Cor 15:9-10). From the time of this experience, Paul could (and was obligated to) proclaim that God had delivered his Son over to death for Jews and Gentiles and raised him from the dead so that they might be declared just at the final judgment (cf. Rom 4:24-25 with Isa 53:10-12). Therefore, despite their sin and distance from God, they can and shall, through the intercession of the exalted Christ, be justified before the judgment throne of God "by faith (alone) apart from observing the law" (cf. Rom 3:28 and 8:34).

2.2.2 According to 2 Cor 5:21; Rom 3:21-26 and 10:3-4, the Christology of the apostle and his doctrine of justification are (almost) identical, and in both cases the subject is the establishment of God's righteousness in and through Christ, which creates salvation and benevolent order. The Pauline teaching about Christ, who represents God's righteousness, holiness and redemption for those who believe (1 Cor 1:30), thus obtains the comprehensive breadth which the disciples of Paul in Colossians and Ephesians attempted to express with the phrase "God's plan of salvation" (οἰκονομία τοῦ θεοῦ; cf. Col 1:25; Eph 1:10; 3:2, 9): The one God, who created the world and chose Israel to be his own people, proclaimed in advance the coming of the Messiah through the prophets. When the time had fully come, he sent his (pre-existent) Son into the world (Gal 4:4); in accordance with the promise of 2 Sam 7:12-14, this Son descended from the house of David, and started upon his path of sacrifice, which ended upon a cross at Golgotha. After the burial, he was raised from the dead on the third day and declared "Son of God in power," (Rom 1:1-4), taking his place at God's right hand. Salvation at the end time is guaranteed to Jews and Gentiles in him and through him (Rom 3:21-26, 30). He must, however, continue his reign in heaven till all enemies are conquered and God's reign has been initiated (1 Cor 15:25). When all those nations determined by God to do so have entered into the community of salvation, He will appear Himself from Zion to redeem "all Israel" as well from unbelief (Rom 11:25-31). Only then will the age of the "glorious freedom of the children of God" dawn amidst the creation, which will have been freed from its vanity (cf. Rom 8: 20-21; 1 Cor 15:26). It is not difficult to recognize that the structures of this plan of salvation are taken from the Holy Scripture and the Christology of the apostle and is intended to be understood as the eschatological fulfillment of messianic promises.

2.3 Taking their place alongside the Synoptic Gospels and the letters of Paul as central books of the New Testament are the Johannine writings.

2.3.1 Although the relationship between Revelation, the three letters of John, and the Gospel of John, produced by the school (in Asia Minor) of John (the Presbyter), can only be broadly outlined, there can be no doubt that the overriding Biblical theological contribution of the Gospel of John, the Johannine letters, and the Revelation of John is the formation of the Logos-Christology. This is displayed by the Johannine writings in three ways:

2.3.1.1 The oldest layer with regard to its tradition history is most probably found in the apocalyptic description of the exalted Christ in Rev 19:11-16(21), who appears at the head of the armies of heaven in order that he defeat the nations which have rebelled against God. His name is ὁ λόγος τοῦ θεοῦ (Rev 19:13). He is given this name, because he rises up against the enemies of God to establish the righteous will of God with the sword of his mouth.

2.3.1.2 In 1 John 1:1, the preexistent Christ, who was sent by the Father and appeared upon the earth, is called "the word of life" (ὁ λόγος τῆς ζωῆς). He is called this, because he provides (eternal) life and forms the center of the message which John must proclaim.

2.3.1.3 That layer of the Logos-Christology which was most influential for its later development is found in John 1:1-18, the prologue of the Gospel of John. In the Christological hymn, on which the prologue is very likely based, Christ is called simply ὁ λόγος and is thus identified with God's word at creation. The Christ-title expresses that God communicates himself to the world as creator and savior only in and through His only Son, and that the world can encounter God only in and through the person of this Son (cf.1:18 with 14:6). The main Christological interest of the hymn lies in emphasizing the consubstantiality of God and the Logos and in the confession of his incarnation.

The highly developed theological reflection of the Johannine school in John 1:1-18 is evident in the arrangement of the Christological hymn into a three-part prologue to the Gospel of John in which the different reactions of the world to the Logos are expressed: In John 1:1-5, the existence and work of the Logos before, during and after the creation of the world are described. Then, in John 1:6-8, John the Baptist is introduced as the earthly forerunner of the Christ-Logos. Following this, the coming of the Logos into the world is reported in two different ways: The theme of 1:9-13 is the appearance and *rejection* of the Logos in the world, which is prototypically represented by Israel; only a small minority recognizes him to be the revealer and gain through him the status of children of God (cf. 1:12-13). John 1:14-18 speaks of the appearance of the Logos on earth and *recognition* of him by the believers. They confess in 1:14-18 that the Logos became flesh, lived among them and, in contrast to Moses, actually revealed the grace and glory of God. Thus, the prologue of John views the appearance of the Logos in the world as a salvation event which leads to the divorce of light from darkness, belief from unbelief. Through the confession by believers of the Logos in 1:14-18 in the first person plural, the boundary between his pre-Easter and post-Easter work is broken through, and a fundamental tenet of the Johannine Christology becomes visible: The Gospel does not just witness to the saving acts and the history of Jesus, but also, and above all, to the exalted Christ, who is present in the world through his Spirit and the preaching of those who witness to him in the world. In this way, people of all times may be introduced to faith in the Logos and receive eternal life through him (cf. John 20,31).

3. *Result*

The witness to Christ in the letters of Paul is formulated much differently than that in the Johannine writings, but they still have basically *the same message*: God revealed himself to the world only in and through his Son Jesus Christ; only through the way of sacrifice and the resurrection of this Christ did the salvation of the end times become available to Jews and Gentiles; the only way to this salvation is through faith in him, and this faith includes the confession to Jesus as Lord as well as the carrying out of his commands (cf. Gal 5:6; 1 John 4:7-10; John 13:34-35).

4. *Outlook*

In the New Testament, the Holy Scriptures (of the Old Testament) are considered prophecy, inspired by the Holy Spirit, which are to be interpreted by relating them to God's eschatological act of salvation in and through Christ (cf. Rom 15:4; 2 Tim 3:16; Heb 3:7; 10:15 etc.). The key to understanding them is the gospel concerning Jesus Christ, in whom God has revealed himself once and for all (Rom 1:1-6; 1 Pet 1:10-12; Heb 1:1-2). In apostolic times, as the Gospels were produced, the Revelation of John written, and the letters of Paul collected, the theory of inspiration was extended to cover the New Testament books (cf. John 21:24; Rev 22:18-19; 2 Pet 1:20-21; 3:16). Since the second century they form, together with the γραφαὶ ἅγιαι, the two-part canon of the Christian Bible. They cannot, nor do they intend, to replace the Old Testament, but they do testify to God's definitive and final revelation in Jesus Christ and show how the "Holy Scriptures" are to be put into relation with this revelation.

Because both parts of the canon are inspired by the Holy Spirit, the hermeneutics of the Church have been based on the same principle to which the Reformers also adhered: "The Holy Scripture must be read and interpreted in the same Spirit in which it was written."[11] This principle is valid today, and it especially deserves hermeneutical consideration when one attempts to construct a Biblical Theology of the New Testament in which the biblical texts are to be interpreted in the way in which they want to be interpreted, namely, as inspired witnesses of the path which God in and through Christ took to humanity in order to lead them back to himself and thereby to salvation. Insofar as a Biblical Theology of the (Old and) New Testament(s) describes this path, it lays the foundation for the Church's testimony of faith.

NOTES

1. Cf. B. S. CHILDS, *Biblical Theology of the Old and New Testaments*, 1992, pp. 225-229.

2. CHILDS, ibid. (see n. 1), p. 77.

3. Cf. H. HÜBNER, *Biblische Theologie des Neuen Testaments*, vol. 1, 1990, pp. 57ff.

4. Cf. M. HENGEL, "Die Septuaginta als 'christliche Schriftensammlung' und das Problem ihres Kanons," in *Die Septuaginta zwischen Judentum und Christentum*, (eds.) M. HENGEL and A. M. SCHWEMER, 1994, pp. 182-284 (esp. pp. 241ff., pp. 270ff.).

5. I have pointed out some of these deficiencies in my book, *Vom Verstehen des Neuen Testaments*, 1986², pp. 199-205.

6. H. HÜBNER, *Biblische Theologie*, vol. 1, p. 240 (emphasis his).

7. I am also aware of the fact that I would never have found this way had it not been for the works and advice of HARTMUT GESE, MARTIN HENGEL, and FRIEDRICH MILDENBERGER, and that I cannot traverse this way to its end without their kind criticism.

8. Cf. H. GESE, "Hermeneutische Grundsätze der Exegese biblischer Texte," in his *Alttestamentliche Studien*, 1991, pp. 249-265.

9. Cited according to H. DIEM, *Ja oder Nein*, 1974, p. 290.

10. Since what follows is a summary of that which has been said in the previous chapters concerning the preaching of Jesus, the testimony of Paul and the Johannine school, notes can be dispensed with.

11. Dei Verbum III, 12.

LITERATURE IN BIBLICAL THEOLOGY

1. *General Literature*

Ex Auditu - An International Journal of Theological Interpretation of Scripture. Edited by Klyne R. Snodgrass, Allison Park, Pennsylvania: Pickwick Publications. Vol. 1-, 1985-.

Horizons in Biblical Theology - An International Dialogue. Edited by Ulrich Mauser et al., Pittsburgh: Pittsburgh Theological Seminary. Vol. 1-, 1979-.

Jahrbuch für Biblische Theologie. Edited by Ingo Baldermann et al., Neukirchen: Neukirchener Verlag. Vol. 1-, 1986-.

Feinberg, John S. ed., *Continuity and Discontinuity. Perspectives on the Relationship Between the Old and New Testaments*, Wheaton, Ill.: Crossway Books, 1988, 410 pp.

Fuller, Daniel P. *The Unity of the Bible. Unfolding God's Plan for Humanity.* Grand Rapids: Zondervan Publishing House. 1992, 508 pp.

Reumann, John, ed. *The Promise and Practice of Bibical Theology.* Minneapolis: Fortress Press, 1991, 214 pp.

Reventlow, Henning Graf. *Problems of Biblical Theology in the Twentieth Century.* ET Philadelphia: Fortress Press, 1986.

Smart, James D. *The Past, Present, and Future of Biblical Theology.* Philadelphia: Westminster Press, 1979, 162 pp.

Terrien, Samuel. *The Elusive Presence. Toward a New Biblical Theology.* San Francisco: Harper & Row, 1978, 511 pp.

Van Gemeren, Willem. *The Progress of Redemption. The Story of Salvation from Creation to the New Jerusalem.* Grand Rapids: Zondervan Publishing House, 1988, 544 pp.

Vos, Geerhardus. *Biblical Theology*. Grand Rapids: Wm. B. Eerdmans Publishing Co., 1948, 426 pp.

Wright, G. Ernest. *God Who Acts, Biblical Theology as Recital*. Studies in Biblical Theology, No. 8. London: SCM Press, 1952, 132 pp.

2. *Old Testament*

Barr, James. *Old and New in Interpretation*. London: SCM Press, 1966.

Childs, Brevard S. *Biblical Theology of the Old and New Testaments: Theological Reflection on the Christian Bible*. Minneapolis: Fortress Press, 1993, 745 pp.

Dumbrell, William J. *Covenant and Creation. An Old Testament Covenantal Theology*. Nashville: Thomas Nelson Publishers, 1984, 217 pp.

Freedman, David Noel. *The Unity of the Hebrew Bible*. Ann Arbor: University of Michigan Press, 1991.

Gese, Hartmut. *Essays on Biblical Theology*, ET. Minne-apolis: Augsburg Publishing House, 1981, 256 pp.

Hanson, Paul D. *The Diversity of Scripture*. Philadelphia: Fortress Press, 1982.

Rad, Gerhard von. *Theology of the Old Testament*, 2 Vols., ET. Edinburgh and New York: I, 1963, 483 pp.; II, 1965, 470 pp.

Wyschogrod, Michael. *The Body of Faith. Judaism as Corporeal Election*. Minneapolis, 1983.

3. *New Testament*

Beasley-Murray, G. R. *Jesus and the Kingdom of God*. Grand Rapids: Wm. B.Eerdmans Co., 1986, 446 pp.

Betz, Otto. *What Do We Know about Jesus?* ET. London: SCM Press, 1968, 126 pp.

Cullmann, Oscar. *Christ and Time. The Primitive Christian Conception of Time and History.* ET Philadelphia: Westminster Press, 1964.

Ellis, E. Earle. "Jesus' Use of the Old Testament and the Genesis of New Testament Theology," in: *Bulletin for Biblical Research* 3 (1993): pp. 59-75.

Ellis, E. Earle. *Prophecy and Hermeneutic in Early Christianity. New Testament Essays, WUNT* 18, Tübingen: Mohr, 1978 (reprint: Grand Rapids 1978), 289 pp.

Ellis, E. Earle. *The Old Testament in Early Christianity. Canon and Interpretation in the Light of Modern Research, WUNT* 54, Tübingen: Mohr, 1991, 188 pp.

Goppelt, Leonhard. *Theology of the New Testament.* 2 vols. ET Grand Rapids: Wm. B. Eerdmans Publishing Co., I, 1981, II 1982.

Hengel, Martin. *Between Jesus and Paul: Studies in the Earliest History of Christianity.* ET Philadelphia: Fortress Press, 1983, 220 pp.

Hengel, Martin. *The Atonement: A Study of the Origins of the Doctrine in the New Testament.* ET London: SCM Press, 1981, 112 pp.

Hengel, Martin. *The Johannine Question.* ET London: SCM Press, 1989, 240 pp.

Jeremias, Joachim. *New Testament Theology. The Proclamation of Jesus.* ET New York: Charles Scribner's Sons, 1971.

Kümmel, Werner G. *The Theology of the New Testament According to Its Major Witnesses: Jesus—Paul—John.* ET Nashville: Abingdon Press, 1973.

Ladd, George E. *A Theology of the New Testament,* Revised Edition. Edited by D. A. Hagner. Grand Rapids: Wm. B. Eerdmans Publishing Co., 1993.

Schweizer, Eduard. *Jesus the Parable of God. What do we really know about Jesus?* Allison Park, Pennsyvania: Pickwick Publications, 1994.

Stuhlmacher, Peter. "The Gospel of Reconciliation in Christ. Basic Features and Issues of a Biblical Theology of the New Testament," in: *Horizons in Biblical Theology*. Vol. 1, 1979, pp. 161-190.

Stuhlmacher, Peter. *Reconciliation, Law, and Righteousness, Essays in Biblical Theology*. ET Philadelphia: Fortress Press, 1986, 200 pp.

Stuhlmacher, Peter. Biblische Theologie des Neuen Testaments. Vol. 1, *Grundlegung: Von Jesus zu Paulus*, Göttingen: Vandenhoeck & Ruprecht, 1992, 419 pp. ET Forthcoming with Wm. B. Eerdmans Publishing Co., Grand Rapids: Michigan.

Stuhlmacher, Peter. *Paul's Letter to the Romans*. ET Louisville: Westminster: John Knox Press, 1994, 269 pp.

Stuhlmacher. Peter. *Jesus of Nazareth—Christ of Faith*, ET Peabody, Mass.: Hendrickson, 1993, 109 pp.

Wright, N. Tom. *The Climax of the Covenant*, Edinburgh: T&T Clark, 1991.

Wright, N. Tom. *The New Testament and the People of God. Christian Origins and the Question of God*, Vol. 1, Minneapolis: Fortress Press, 1992.

Wright, N. Tom. *Jesus and the Victory of God. Christian Origins and the Question of God*, vol 2, Minneapolis: Fortress Press, 1994.

4. *Systematic Theology*

Bayer, Oswald. *Theologie*, Gütersloh: Gütersloher Verlagshaus, 994, 548 pp.

Mildenberger, Friedrich. *Biblische Dogmatik: Eine biblische Theologie in dogmatischer Perspektive*, 3 vols., Stuttgart/Berlin/Köln: W. Kohlhammer GmbH, 1991-1993.

Wainwright, Geoffrey. *Doxology*. New York: Oxford University Press, 1980.

5. *Critical Opinions*

Morgan, Robert with John Barton. *Biblical Interpretation,* Oxford: University Press, 1988.

Räisänen, Heikki. *Beyond New Testament Theology.* Philadelphia: Trinity Press, 1990.

Strecker, Georg. "Biblische Theologie?" in: *Kirche. Festschrift für Günther Bornkamm zum 75. Geburtstag,* eds. D. Lührmann and G. Strecker, Tübingen: J. C. B. Mohr-Verlag, 1980, pp. 425-445.